Salvation Today

Yushi*

Salvation Today

Pauline Webb

SCM PRESS LTD

For my father

Nunc dimittis . . .

334 01434 4

First published 1974
by SCM Press Ltd
56 Bloomsbury Street, London

© SCM Press Ltd 1974

Typeset by Gloucester Typesetting Co Ltd
Printed in Great Britain by
Offset Lithography by
Billing & Sons Ltd
Guildford and London

Contents

Acknowledgments

I am grateful to the Rev. Dr Philip Potter and the staff of the World Council of Churches, who organized the Bangkok Conference, for their help and their readiness to make available the documents associated with the Conference, many of which are quoted in this book. I acknowledge also the great help given by Mr Martin Conway of the Publications Office who read the manuscript and made many helpful suggestions for its improvement. I also owe a debt of gratitude to Mrs Mary Riley who by keeping pace with me in typing the manuscript urged me on to endure to the end! Acknowledgment is made for permission to quote copyright material. World Council of Churches documents, the *International Review of Mission* and *Risk* may all be obtained either direct from the WCC, 150, Route de Ferney, Geneva 1120, Switzerland or through the BCC Office, 10 Eaton Gate, London SW1.

Preface

In a shabby upper room not far from Westminster Abbey a group of people had gathered for their usual weekly meeting. They were a motley crowd oddly mixed in age and class and yet greeting one another with a familiarity which suggested a strong common bond between them. Many of them had been coming to this room regularly every week for five or six years with a zeal rarely matched by the most ardent church-goers. The link between their meeting and any church was a tenuous one – the meetings owed their origin to the initiative of a Methodist minister, but most of those who attended would only be seen dead in a church! During their lifetime they looked for support instead to this group all of whom to some extent shared the same problems and were seeking the same solutions. They were all gripped by a compulsive addiction to gambling and were trying to help one another to wrench themselves free from its grasp.

Meetings of Gamblers' Anonymous take a ritual form. The main part of the evening is the telling of 'therapies' (religious people would call them 'testimonies'), giving the story of a group member's experience. On this occasion a man was recalling how his life had been ruined by his addiction – he had robbed, been imprisoned, lost his job, become estranged from his wife. His world had gone to pieces. Then he had found his way to this upper room where he sensed a new attitude towards him. He described it as something that enabled him to look people straight in the eye. He did not know what to call it – compassion was perhaps the best word because here were people who really had been through it with him. They had helped him to work out a way of repaying his debts, to find another job, to be reconciled to his wife, to get a new purpose for living – in other words, to put his life together again. 'My life was shattered and I was in the gutter,' he said, 'and they picked up the pieces and made me stand on my feet again. I can only sum it all up,' he concluded, 'by saying I have been saved.' Then, catching sight of the Methodist minister and founder sitting there he hurried on apologetically, 'I don't mean that word in any religious sense,' he explained, 'I mean I've been *really* saved.'

Religious non-sense or real experience? What do Christians really mean when they talk about salvation? It is with that question that this book begins.

I

You Can Say That Again

An Attempt at Defining 'Salvation'

Words, like coins, become in common currency defaced and indecipherable. To rediscover their full value they need to be re-minted. This book is an attempt at re-minting an old word of the Christian faith, a word whose value in scriptural terms is a treasure-store of connotation and content. But in the hands of street-corner peddlars of evangelism it has sometimes been reduced to a formula empty of worth, offering a private passport to heaven which has no earthly value. Today Christians all over the world are feeling the need to recover this great word of the faith as they look for a shorthand term to express the wholeness of their gospel. People looking for meaning in personal and social experience, people searching for a sense of individual worth and of corporate identity, people seeking release from a sense of guilt or failure, people pursuing values which have both temporal and eternal significance, people concerned about justice and a new order of society, people seeking above all for a sense of wholeness in life, some cohesive purpose holding all things together – all these can be said, in short, to be in search of salvation.

So you can say it again, this great word of the Christian faith. But what does it really mean today? That has been the theme of discussions among Christians across the world

over the past couple of years, culminating in the international conference, held recently in Bangkok, which took
as its title the deceptively simple phrase *Salvation Today*.
Though this book does not set out in any way to be a full
report of that Conference, many of the ideas expressed here
originated there where discussions with people from some
sixty different nations, and even more different churches
and traditions, acted like a kaleidoscope to shake into new
patterns and sharper focus our fragmented glimpses of the
truths entrusted to us in the treasury of the gospel.

The particular significance of the Bangkok Conference
was that the majority of the people there did not come from
the traditional homelands of so-called Christendom. So they
did not look at the gospel as so many Westerners do, as a
veil of religious respectability thrown over the historically
developed forms of European culture, taking its shape from
them; but they saw the gospel instead gleaming in sharp
contrast to the backcloth against which it has so often been
presented to them. Most of them looked critically at the
'salvation systems' of Western society described by the Swiss
poet Kurt Marti:

> This is an upright country
> with clean people
> and with clean salvation systems
> which are all on 'go'
>
> After his birth
> every citizen
> still fidgeting
> is laid on the assembly line
> automatically
> drilled by ceremonies
> until the last one
> lovingly spits him out
> into the fields of elysia
>
> This is an upright country
> with clean people
> with clean salvation systems
> which are all on 'go'[1]

In response, people from the East would quote the words of the Tamil poet, Shanmugha Subbiah in his poem *To the Westerners*.

> On the one hand you devise
> Ways of living well;
> on the other you dig
> graves with consummate knowledge[2]

They looked rather for a gospel that would save mankind from everything that dehumanizes people and would restore us all to the dignity of our full humanity, as we see that humanity made in the image of Christ. Writing of the impact of the Christian gospel on India, M. M. Thomas, Director of the Christian Institute for the Study of Religion and Society in Bangalore, says:

> Where conversion was genuine whether individuals or groups, the converts saw salvation in Christ not only in terms of individual salvation or heaven after death, but also as the spiritual source of a new community on earth in which their human dignity and status were recognized. It was the promise of humanization inherent in the gospel of salvation that led to the influx of the oppressed into the church. It was the same promise in Christ's salvation of a richer and fuller human life for all men in society and of a new community of freedom and love that attracted some of the intellectuals of the privileged classes in India and brought them to acknowledge Christ as their Lord and God.[3]

Salvation is to do with humanization. To say this does not in any way diminish the gospel of Christ; rather it magnifies the humanity whom Christ came to save. By humanization Christians mean everything which helps men and women to grow to their full stature, measured by the humanity of Christ himself. For a Christian that will include an eager desire to make known the good news that Christ has opened up to all people the way to that perfection. His perfection comes from God, and all that is imperfect in humanity originates in turning away from God and from his purposes for mankind. So to say that salvation is to do with humanization is not to deny that salvation is about the ways of God

3

with man; it is rather to affirm that the struggles of men everywhere for their humanity are integrally related to the gospel of God's acts of salvation.

Those who proclaim the good news that in the life, death and resurrection of Jesus of Nazareth, God acted to save the world do so in a world that seems bent on its own destruction. To proclaim the gospel must also mean to join in the battle against those destructive forces, whether they be the evils within a person's own heart or the principalities and powers of evil that seem to dominate the very fabric of the world's life and infect all human institutions. As the Report of the Section on Renewal in Mission at the Uppsala Assembly of the World Council of Churches put it:

> We belong to a humanity that cries passionately and articulately for a fully human life. Yet the very humanity of man and his societies is threatened by a greater variety of destructive forces than ever. And the acutest moral problems all hinge upon the question: What is man? . . . There is a burning relevance today in describing the mission of God in which we participate as the gift of a new creation which is a radical renewal of the old and the invitation to men to grow up into their full humanity in the new man, Jesus Christ. [4]

The new man Jesus is God incarnate. To grow up into him therefore means first to grow in the knowledge and love of God who has made humanity in his own image. The new man Jesus is also the man for others. To grow up in him means also therefore to grow in the knowledge and love of one's fellow man, with whom everyone shares a common humanity. Love of God and love of neighbour are the hallmarks of true humanization. To lack either is to be incompletely human.

So the process of humanization begins for the Christian with telling, celebrating and re-enacting the story of what God has done to restore man to his true image. In his living, dying and rising again Jesus showed the way in which mankind can be saved from all that distorts humanity, even from death itself. It is this humanity of God revealed in Jesus which makes plain to us the inhumanity of man. It is his perfection which becomes the mirror in which we see our

4

imperfections. It is his promise of salvation which gives us back our hope, that however realistic we may be about the evil that seems to dominate the human heart and the cosmic powers, we live always in the possibility of a redeemed humanity and a restored creation.

So Christians can afford to be realists, to recognize that all human systems have their ugly face and yet to behold the glory of God and of man in the face of Jesus Christ. In him we are made aware of how far short we fall of the measure of our full humanity. 'Falling short of the mark' is a literal translation of Paul's word for 'sin'. Recognizing sin for what it is, naming sins in their particular form, is another essential process of humanization. Too often Christians have defined sin solely in personal terms. But if we think of sin as everything that dehumanizes, whether it be idolatory that prevents man from loving God, or injustice that prevents him from loving his neighbour, or pride that destroys his true selfhood, or prejudice that robs his brother of his birthright, or selfishness that poisons his personal life, or greed that infects his whole economy, we see that sin is both individual and corporate, personal and public, arising from the depths of the human heart and built into the very structure of human society. Jesus came both to save each person from his sin and to take away the sins of the world.

If all people are to see this salvation, then the way of the Lord must be prepared by those who already live under the reign of his Kingdom. That preparation is both personal and political. It is a very practical and humane advice that John the Baptist gives to those who respond to his call to repent: 'And the multitudes asked him, "What then shall we do?" And he answered them, "He who has two coats, let him share with him who has none; and he who has food, let him do likewise." Tax collectors also came to be baptized, and said to him, "Teacher, what shall we do?" And he said to them, "Collect no more than is appointed you." Soldiers also asked him, "And we, what shall we do?" And he said to them, "Rob no one by violence or by false accusation, and be content with your wages" ' (Luke 3.10–14).

5

Such radical change of conduct would mean a real right-about-turn, a re-thinking of human goals and destiny, a repentance, and it is repentance that opens the way to salvation. Salvation, then, includes all that is meant by humanization, though it goes far beyond it. It means all this and heaven too! It recognizes realistically that the wages of sin is death, but it offers to mankind the gift of God which is eternal life, life abundantly human, life that cannot be destroyed even by death itself, life lived under the rule of God which brings all other rules into question, life that gives meaning by love which forgives the sin of the past and opens up new hope for the future.

This definition of salvation as humanization needs further filling out. At the Bangkok Conference, people from many different situations tried to define salvation in terms of their experience. We were offered many proposed definitions:

> During the last twenty years we have discovered that salvation has to do with political and economic aspects of life (a Latin American).

> Salvation is in Jesus Christ where we find all freedom, whether we are prisoners, captives or oppressed by any nation. If we have that depth of spirituality in Jesus Christ then we shall find that freedom in him which is our salvation (a Fijian).

> In our context salvation would mean freedom from colonial powers, our independence (an African).

> Salvation is a fact and we share it in the name of Jesus Christ through the holy eucharist (a Greek).

> I see the great need to consider salvation in terms of communities and nations. I find my individual salvation in so far as I'm able to work for the salvation of my people and our country (a Sri Lankan).

> In the Bible the basic element in salvation is the reconciliation of man who as a sinner is separated from God, is restored to the fellowship with God on account of that sacrifice which Jesus Christ wrought for us on his cross (a German).

> Being an artist, being able to go from one day to the next not knowing exactly where the day's going to take you, where your

art's going to take you, it seems to me that this has to do with salvation, that this is my salvation. This is it (an American).

Salvation is many different things because it comes into existence in many situations. To the blind man whom Jesus healed salvation was healing; to the man on the cross salvation was coming to Paradise. And today if the whole world is threatened by war, then salvation consists in peace. If people are overcome by guilt and suffering, salvation means forgiveness and liberation from this guilt (a Dane).

Such diverse definitions could confuse us. A word can be given so many meanings that it comes to have no meaning at all. It is as well at this stage to recall what the word salvation originally meant.

The Rev. Dr Philip Potter, General Secretary of the World Council of Churches, is an enthusiastic student of etymology. Speaking at the second triennial assembly of the Canadian Council of Churches a few weeks before the Bangkok Conference, he directed attention to the root meanings of the word 'salvation' in the three languages that were current at the time of Jesus – Hebrew, Greek and Latin.

The very name of Jesus (the one who saves) is derived from the Hebrew verb *yasha* which means to be wide, spacious, ample. The noun *Yeshua* means the state of being wide and spacious, of being liberated and free. No longer are 'the saved' hemmed in by enemies, earthly, cosmic or demonic. No longer are they handicapped by distress or misfortune of any kind. They are liberated *from* all that impedes and liberated *for* all that makes for well-being, outward and inward. The state of salvation is one in which crops grow and flocks flourish, in which order and peace prevail in the state. Individuals and communities are set free to become their real selves, to pursue the life intended for them by God. Freed alike from sin and rebellion, from disaster and disarray, from wrong attitudes and enemy attacks, from misguided policies and mistaken actions, each person and the whole community, integrally bound together, attain that state of wellbeing on which the health of the whole society depends, a health which derives from the

7

God who saves because he is the truly free, unhampered, generous, reliable One.

The Greek work for salvation is *soteria*. Dr Potter finds this word being used with four primary meanings in Greek literature current at the time of Jesus. First, there is salvation or deliverance from ill-health and the saviour is the god Asklepius; second, there is deliverance from the perils of the sea and the saviours are the gods, the Dioskouri; third, there is deliverance from imprisonment in the physical body and in the material world, which are bound to die, and from which one is liberated for immortality; this concept is stressed in the mystery religions and focused in the 'saviour' gods Isis and Serapis; fourth, there is the idea found among the philosophers of salvation as liberation from ignorance, false opinions and suspicions. The title saviour itself (*soter*) was used of Roman emperors and other political leaders. One of the titles of the Roman emperor was 'Saviour of the World' – significantly used in the New Testament as a title of Jesus, a challenge to the false saviours that the emperors were.

In Latin the word *salvatio* originates from the word *salus* which means authenticity, integrity, genuineness, fullness. To be in a state of *salus* (as we would express in a greeting or salute) means being sound, safe, healthy, all of a piece. It means being an authentic person, truly and integrally oneself, free from all that impedes one's growth.

Where is such an authentic, real, fully realized human being to be found? Dr Potter points us to Matthew's gospel, which begins by defining the name of the one who came to reveal salvation – to be the true man, Jesus. His name means he who saves, he who in the freedom of his existence for others sets them free to be real persons like himself, if they will commit themselves to him. This is no shadow of a human being. Matthew gives substance and identity to him at the very beginning of his gospel. This is Jesus who is the Son of David and the Son of Abraham. He has a clear historic identity and a defined cultural background. To be truly human means to share an identity and to inherit a culture, but never to be imprisoned by them. Jesus comes to

8

fulfil and to transcend his inheritance. 'He is', in Dr Potter's words, 'a son of his culture but not a slave to it.' He exemplifies the capacity of human beings to transcend their situation, to be both part of their past and free for the future. He is both Son of David – in a proud and patriotic descent – and also Son of Abraham, the one who broke the bounds of his culture and nation and became the nomad, the pilgrim. In Abraham all families of the earth are blessed. The Hebrew word for blessing, as Dr Potter again points out, is *barakh*, sharing one's strength and life with another, being with him. In Abraham all families of the earth will share a common life, drawing upon a shared strength and discovering unity in the midst of their diversity.

Jesus too ventures beyond the bounds of his class and his nation as he went out to those beyond the pale of normal society – to the outcast, the rejected, the despised people of his day. Indeed it is in these very outsiders that Jesus tells us we can identify him and recognize his presence. And as we minister to them we find our identity also. 'We discover our humanity', says Dr Potter, 'as we seek to affirm the humanity of others.'

Another way of trying to get at the meaning of the word salvation is to look at the way it is used in our own time outside Christian circles. The Chinese, for example, had no word to express the concept of saviour. Early Bible translators used for the word saviour a word meaning protector and guardian, a word associated with the word for soldier. Its biblical usage gave it a special connotation, and in Chinese dictionaries it is now referred to as a Christian term. But it is a term which significantly has come into much more common use as people have tried to describe all that Chairman Mao means to the life of the new China. He, the guardian and protector of the people, is also seen as their saviour. Only the word that Christians traditionally used of Jesus is adequate to express the debt of gratitude which Chinese people feel for the one who inaugurated the great revolution. So to Chairman Mao are written hymns of salvation, describing his achievements in China in terms reminiscent of the prophets' description of the saving work of the Messiah in the new Israel. Compare the following contemporary hymn of salvation in China with a Christian hymn of salvation. In the Chinese hymn, the human liberator is almost deified by his people; in the Christian hymn the divinely anointed one is hailed as the human liberator of all mankind.

> Chairman Mao, dear Chairman Mao,
> Truth's embodiment you are, the light of dawn,
> Mankind's saving star, hope of the world . . .

Compare this with

> Hail the heaven-born Prince of Peace!
> Hail the Sun of Righteousness!
> Light and life to all he brings,
> Risen with healing in his wings.

Various languages have used different kinds of words to express the Christian concept of salvation. In many African languages, the word used is one of rescue, taking out of a dangerous place and putting into a new safe situation. In others it is a word of cleansing, suggesting washing clean in a river. In some Asian languages the word is one of reconciliation, of making peace after a quarrel. In many European languages it is a word related to healing and making whole again. Watching a service for the deaf recently I was quickly able to recognize the gesture for salvation – a gathering in safely into the fold of an embrace.

Significant, too, is the way the word is used in secular speech with no hint of religious association. Even in Bangkok in the heat of the afternoon sun, I heard people claiming that the excellent swimming pool was their salvation which, I am pretty certain, was not meant to be a theological statement about salvation by immersion! We speak of a person or an event that *saves* a situation. What does this really imply? The saving event is usually the one that introduces some new element into an apparently deadlocked situation, a person who makes an unexpected sacrifice, or a new happening that puts everything that has gone before into a different perspective, or a risk taken by one who is prepared to lose everything for the sake of the other. Watch any conflict situation, for example, in a television play or a modern novel and ask, 'Who is the one who saves the situation here? How does he or she help to resolve the conflict?' Often it is the person least expected, the one who seems to be the victim of events rather than the instigator of them, and who yet, by some unexpected initiative, makes those events turn upon a new axis.

But it is always costly. There is no cheap salvation. And the price is usually paid not by the one who is being saved but by someone else on his behalf. Think, for instance, of the classic romantic situation of the triangular relationship which threatens a marriage. Often the marriage can be saved only by the sacrifice of a third person, a sacrifice which may be unknown and will almost certainly be unheralded but which will nevertheless be costly. Or think of the more famed and approved sacrifice whereby men and women lay down their lives in order to save some cause to which they are deeply committed. One of the most moving testimonies in the anthology entitled *Salvation Tody and Contemporary Experience*, which was prescribed preparatory reading for the Bangkok Conference, showed how this kind of saving, sacrificial love restores meaning to life as it sets people free to live and even to die for others. In a *Letter to God* written by a Bolivian guerilla fighter who aligned himself with the struggle of the oppressed as part of his evangelistic obedience to the gospel of Christ, Nestor Paz on the eve of his own death pours out his understanding of what such sacrifice means in a prayer which is reminiscent of the prayer of Jesus himself on the eve of his pouring out his life for all mankind.

Dear Lord,
It has been a long time since I wrote to you. Today I feel a real need for you and your presence, perhaps because of the nearness of death or the relative failure of the struggle. You know that I have tried to be faithful to you – always and by all means – consistent with my whole being. That is why I am here. I understand love as the urgency of helping to solve the problems of the 'other person' – in whom you are present.

I left what I had and came here. Perhaps today is my (Maundy) Thursday and tonight my (Good) Friday. Because I love you I surrender everything I am into your hands, without limit. What hurts me is the thought of leaving those I most love – Cecy and my family – and perhaps not being here to participate in the triumph of the people – their liberation.

We are a group full of true 'Christian' humanity, and I think we will change the course of history. The thought of this comforts me. I love you and I give you myself and ourselves, completely, because you are my Father. No one's death is meaningless if his life has been charged with significance; and I believe this has been true of us, here.

Chau, Lord! Perhaps until that heaven of yours, that new world we desire so much!

'Greater love has no man than this,' said Jesus, 'that a man lay down his life for his friends.' Such a saving love can dare even to look death in the face, in the confidence that not even death can destroy our true humanity. Our earthly life is lived always under the menace of death, the permanent question mark posed over the meaning of every human story. The full meaning can be finally affirmed only beyond the grave. It needed some one to break through the death barrier to bring back to us the confidence that the last great enemy has been overcome. The triumphant affirmation of Christians is that Jesus has done just that. He has died our death and from the other side of the grave he has brought us back our hope that with him and in him our humanity shall find its final and eternal salvation.

So we come back to the definition with which we began. Salvation is to do with humanization. To be fully free, authentic persons, we need to penetrate beyond the present limits of our existence, to break through the bounds of all that confines our humanity, even through death itself.

'In Jesus', wrote Karl Barth, 'the fact is once for all established that God does not exist without man. God is human.' In him too is established the fact that man cannot exist without God. Man is made in his image. Salvation is the restoring of that image, the reconciliation of all that humanity is with all that God meant it to be. The way to that salvation is Jesus. There is no other name for it. You can say that again.

2

Beginning at the End

Salvation to Our God Who Sits on the Throne

Salvation is not an idea but a story. Any study of salvation must begin with that book full of stories – the Bible.

Those people who cannot withstand the temptation to peep at the back of a book before they start on its story often stumble on a startling clue which changes the whole perspective in which they read the rest. That would certainly be true for anyone who began at the back of the Bible. The revelation there comes with the shock of a disclosure underlying the mystery of all the other books. If we begin at the beginning of the Bible, we might well imagine that these books are to be about God's dealings with man, God working out his plan of salvation for the world which he created and which man comes near to destroying but which will never finally elude God's good design. Begin at the end, and the whole thing seems to be turned around: the theme of the book of Revelation is not man's salvation but God's! 'Salvation to our God' shout the triumphant hosts in heaven (Rev. 7.10). Even the translators find this concept difficult to cope with. Some modern versions try to get round it by rendering the Greek dative as 'Salvation comes from our God', which is what we might expect the redeemed sinners to proclaim. But this translation is difficult to defend in view of the fact that the Greek construction in v. 10 is exactly the same as in v. 12, where there is no doubt that praise and glory and wisdom and thanksgiving and honour are being rendered *to* God and do not just emanate *from* hom. We need to think again about what it means to suggest that the Bible is the story of a God in need of salvation.

The very suggestion affronts us. For to most of us the concept of God is in itself synonymous with the idea of omnipotence. Despite all the doubts that assail us when prayer seems unanswered, despite the feeling that this is a God-forsaken universe, despite the fact that we live most of our lives as though God were absent rather than present, we still cling to the faith that he could answer any prayer if only we asked properly. He will never let man have the last word and end the world with a bang or a whimper, He is keeping an eye on us all the time. So all we need to do to be saved is to repeat the right formulae or liturgy, to give up the idea that we have a free will, and to surrender every part of our lives to an almighty power which can propel us along in predetermined paths towards our eternal destiny.

But what if we were wrong? In one of the readings selected for the anthology on *Salvation Today and Contemporary Experience*, Marguerite Yourcenar asks that very question through the words of a Prior conversing with a Renaissance philosopher and scientist:

> What if we are mistaken in postulating that God is all-powerful, and in supposing our woes to be the result of His will? What if it is for us to establish His Kingdom on earth? I have said to you before that God delegates Himself; now I go beyond that, Sebastian. Possibly He is only a small flame in our hands, and we alone are the ones to feed and keep this flame alight; perhaps we are the farthest point to which He can advance . . . How many sufferers who are incensed when we speak of an almighty God would rush from the depth of their own distress to succour Him in His frailty if we asked them to do so? . . .
>
> We are indeed weak, each one of us, but there is some consolation in the thought that He may be even weaker than we, and more discouraged still, and that it is our task to beget Him and save Him in all living beings . . .[1]

God delegates himself. From the moment when he walks in the garden with Adam and hands over to him the creatures he has designed so that Adam might name them and tame them, and subdue the earth to man's will, till the moment when he ascends the throne of his glory in the guise of the gentlest of those creatures, a lamb that has been slain, God lays aside his power and depends upon man for his own history as well as for the history of mankind.

Anne-Marie Aagaard of Denmark puts it this way:

God himself has a history, and man's history on earth affects God's history. God will become what he was not before, when salvation finally will belong to him in the Kingdom. Now he suffers, and 'until the earth grows into a Kingdom' he is a God in need of salvation, because the history of his Kingdom is created only by the power of love and suffering of the crucified Christ *and* crucified man (cf. Rev. 12.10) . . . [Our Conference at Bangkok] was led from a preoccupation with *our* salvation in our varied histories to the quest for a theology of salvation which has God's own history, his suffering in Christ and the final vindication of *his* salvation as the *cantus firmus* . . . [God] is only omnipotent in love, and as long as his will is contradicted by the history of evil on earth he is not yet the God who he will become when all evil has been eradicated 'by the sacrifice of the lamb and by the testimony which they uttered; for they did not hold their lives too dear to lay them down' (Rev. 12.11). Only from then onwards will salvation belong to our God, and the power uncontradicted be the power of the Messiah.[2]

Omnipotent only in love. Is this the clue then to that strange contradictory story of Paradise lost and Exodus achieved, of law pronounced and sin forgiven, of anointed king and angry prophet, of exile and return; of a stable-birth and an angel-song, of a criminal's cross and an empty tomb, of a power-filled church and the persecuted saints? Is the one consistent theme in all these inconsistencies that God can do only that which love makes possible and that he is vindicated only by realizing fully his own nature which is wholly love? So God himself is saved – wholly authenticated, fully realized; and we are saved as we share in that salvation, as we too consistently live, as Philip Potter would say, 'not by the love of power but by the power of love'. Mother Julian of Norwich saw this in the *Revelations of Divine Love* which came to her just six hundred years ago and she expresses it thus:

You would know our Lord's meaning in this thing? Know it well. Love was his meaning. Who showed it you? Love. What did he show you? Love. Why did he show it? For love. Hold on to this and you will know and understand love more and more. But you will not know or learn anything else – ever . . . I saw for certain, both here and elsewhere, that before ever he made us, God loved us; and that his love has never slackened nor ever shall. In this love all his works have been done, and in this love he has made everything serve us; and in this love our life is everlasting. Our beginning was when we were made, but the love in which he made us never had beginning. In it we have our beginning.[3]

It is this consistency of love that makes sense of the centrality of the cross in Christian experience of salvation. Here we see placarded before us the powerlessness of God – the One who has saved others cannot save himself. Watching that fearful, God-forsaken moment of dereliction on the cross we are tempted to rail against God as the thief does in Sydney Carter's song:

> It's God they ought to crucify
> Instead of you and me
> I said to the man a-hanging on the tree.[4]

It is significant that this song has been called blasphemous by those who are affronted by the very notion of an omnipotent God being blamed for what looks on the face of it an outrageous failure to use his power to justify his goodness. What they miss is the truth that this is God being crucified – being crucified by his consistency to his own nature which can be justified only by love. It is Jesus who is saved by the cross, who is fully justified there, because there his love is unlimited, his life poured out. Only after such a death and defeat can come the shouts of victory to the Lamb upon the throne. His death is as much a part of the victory as his resurrection, for by his death he has been saved – kept whole, maintained his integrity, been totally consistent – and by his resurrection that salvation is joyfully vindicated.

One of the most simple presentations of this view on the cross comes in the current musical *Godspell* where the profound truth comes through in the short, stark phrases of the Finale. Throughout the show we have watched Jesus as the clown romping through life, turning its normally accepted values topsy-turvey, laughing at the pomposity of its authority figures, offering people his incredibly new way of living by love. Then comes the clash and the gay, folksy tunes we have enjoyed until that moment give way to cacophonous discords as the nails crash into his hands and feet. Above the searing music we hear his plaintive cry, 'O God I'm dying . . . O God I'm dead', words echoed by his bewildered, simple-minded band of friends who stumble upon profound truth as they simply cry together, 'O God, you're dead.' God is dead – a phrase so expressive of contemporary experience.

There follows a funeral lament as the friends carry the dead body of Jesus down from the cross, away from the stage, out into the audience. It is almost a sigh of nostalgic longing at first – long live God, long live God – the deep unuttered prayer of our generation. Then dawns the realization of what it is they are singing – those three words are not a lament, but an affirmation. They turn into a shout of triumph echoing the songs of the saints in the Book of Revelation – *Long live God – Salvation to our God*. Only when we have grasped that truth, that the reality of God has been saved for us, that out of his death he has come through to a new life for us all, only then can we, in the final and opening words of *Godspell*, 'prepare the way of the Lord' among a people seeking salvation.

The way of the Lord is the way of the cross – there is no other way to salvation. But what does this mean in terms of our salvation, as we have tried to define that word, our liberation, our being brought to our full humanity? In all generations, that cross has made its own message plain. Over the shrine of Britain's first martyr, St Alban, stands now a great cathedral, its Norman nave still sturdy on massive pillars. On each of those pillars down one side of the cathedral some mediaeval artist has left his paintings, each portraying identical scenes, each placarding for everyone in the cathedral to see the cross of Jesus.

Nowadays each Easter Monday sees thousands of young people flocking to St Albans for a pilgrimage. It is a great

Bank Holiday event including long hikes and picnics on the way, and by the time they come to their service most of the congregation are fairly exhausted. It is not easy to preach to them, and I accepted the invitation to do so last year with considerable trepidation. They gave me my theme – the cost of loving. But what could I say to that vast crowd, 5,000 of them sitting packed tight against one another on the floor of the cathedral? They had been singing songs about the kind of world we live in, a world of hunger and war, of threat and apathy. It struck me that they seemed to be expressing a deep fear of the world and all its problems, a longing to escape to a kind of salvation that would close their eyes to the troubles of the world around them.

It seemed best to begin by looking at the opposite of love – not hatred, but fear. I asked the congregation to show me what fear looked like. Immediately sitting there on the floor they all drew as far apart as they could from one another, hugging themselves tight, shrinking into as small a ball as possible, shutting their eyes close. Then I bade them look up at love, as it was depicted there on the pillars before them – arms stretched out, head held high, body totally exposed in the vulnerability of love. They imitated the posture and as they did so their arms went out to one another, their eyes looked out on the world in which they live and they shouted the name of their salvation – Jesus, Jesus, the One for others, the One who saved them by setting them free from fear, opening them up to the world they live in, liberating them into loving. And the cost of that loving was and always will be the cross.

To claim the salvation of Jesus leads on to the recognition of his Kingdom, power and glory. The word salvation occurs only three times in the Book of Revelation – 7.10; 12.10 and 19.1 – all of them in the context of worship. Salvation is something to sing about, and those who have most right to sing are those who have shared the suffering – the martyr host. They are the ones who have been victims of oppressors, who have suffered under so-called saviours (the Roman emperors), who have seen great empires rise in the apparently unassailable power of Babylon. But they have won through to the victory. They have seen the salvation of the suffering One, so now they can see his Kingdom established, his power upheld. Now they behold his glory and they burst into their hallelujah.

It is the triumph of God's cause that they celebrate, not their own. It is not the faithfulness of the martyrs nor even their assurance of a place in the front row in heaven that is the cause of their rejoicing. In the sheer wonder of worship their own history is transcended, their testimony is only the blood of the Lamb, the life poured out in love. It is like going to a wedding feast. Before the day you may be preoccupied with your own preparations. Have you got the right clothes, have you found an acceptable gift, who else will be there, how will you get on with the other guests? But at the feast itself the focus changes. The questions are silenced. All eyes are on the bride. Her radiance eclipses everyone else's carefully made-up beauty. It is her day, the celebration of her love. So the story ends not with us and with our salvation but with the wedding-feast of the Lamb.

But here we are at the end of the book before we have begun it. Let us get back to the beginning.

3

Back to the Beginning

A Biblical Exploration of Salvation Experiences

Now that we have the clue, we can see who is the real hero
of the stories of salvation with which the Bible begins. He
hides himself at first in the early scenes of human history.
Take the great story which the Jews have always celebrated
as *the* story of salvation – the account of the Exodus from
Egypt. Its first two chapters read almost like a secular
account of a political situation. The situation has arisen
through a population explosion – the descendants of Israel,
which at the time of their descent to Egypt numbered only
seventy, have multiplied so prolifically that a small
group of immigrants has now grown into a nation within
another nation. To the Pharaoh this poses a threat, and he
resolves both to enslave and to control this growing people.
It is hoped that ruthless treatment will diminish them both
in numbers and strength (Ex. 1.10f.). But the effect is the
opposite. The more they are oppressed the more they multi-
ply. So the fanatical tyrant turns to extreme methods –
every male newborn child is to be slain immediately.

Only at this point in the story is the name of God introduced as One who nudges his human agents, the Hebrew
midwives, into a way of saving the newborn children. No
miracles of salvation happen – only a campaign of civil dis-
obedience on the part of a few courageous women. Other

women play their part too – a devoted mother, determined to save her child at all costs, a scheming sister quick to exploit the possibilities in the situation, a disobedient daughter who puts maternal compassion before filial loyalty. The result of their efforts is the emergence of a man who shares their sense of compassion, who is so angered at the sight of people suffering that he strikes out in violence, and who eventually comes to realize that he is himself identified with the oppressed. They are *his* people. Their burden too must be his. Moses has grown up (Ex. 2.11) and now in his mature manhood God is able to make himself known to him as the One who has saved him to be the deliverer of God's people.

In the study of these passages with which we began the Conference at Bangkok, Dr Hans-Ruedi Weber, the leader of the Bible Study, drew our attention to the contrast between these Exodus stories and comparable parallels from ancient Middle Eastern mythology. Of Sargon I of Akkad, the Mesopotamian monarch, who ruled about 2500 BC, it is said that after the secret birth of Sargon his mother (whom some suggest was a virgin priestess of the sun god) put him in a little basket made of reeds and sealed with pitch, and cast the basket upon the river Euphrates. He was found and adopted by Akki, a peasant who drew water, and finally the goddess Ishtar grew fond of him and made him a great and powerful king. And of *Horus*, an Egyptian god, it is said that after the death of the Egyptian god Osiris, his pregnant wife, the mother-goddess Isis, fled the wrath of her brother-in-law Seth, the Egyptian deity of darkness and drought who had killed and mutilated Osiris and was now determined to exterminate also Osiris' son. Isis fled into the impenetrable marshes of the Nile delta, where she gave birth to Horus, the falcon. Hidden among the papyri, (a later version of the myth speaks about a boat of papyrus where Horus was covered by the mat of his nurse, the goddess Nephthys) Seth could not find him. When Horus had grown up he revenged his father and drove his uncle Seth out of Egypt.

The startling contrast between the Exodus narrative and

the other Middle Eastern myths is the natural sequence of human events in the former and the miraculous intervention of divine manipulators in the latter. The story of the Jews' salvation is a story of people, people caught up in the complexities of politics, but people who still manage to find ways of working out their own destinies. Though the tyrant sits on the throne, the little people undermine his strategies and display an undreamed of and unreckoned with power. The secret of that power is in a paradoxical way their powerlessness. They are apparently oppressed, yet they act as secret agents of a hidden God – a fifth column operating in enemy territory. Their God depends upon their ingenuity, their maturity, their consistency, their refusal to allow anyone to set limits on their loving.

Then he reveals his presence to Moses. He is the One who has been active all through the history of his human agents – the God of Abraham, the God of Isaac and the God of Jacob. He is the God who is present now in the midst of the oppressed peoples. He is the One who will be there, whose future will unfold as their story continues – 'I am what I am' he calls himself, in a phrase which can equally well be translated 'I will be what I will be'.

It is this God who has made Moses angry. It is he who has implanted in the heart of an affluent and privileged young man a sense of his identification with the oppressed. It is he who has fired him with the determination to win liberation for his people. But it is he too who pushes beyond that liberation, which must never be seen as an end in itself. The climax of the story of Moses is not the crossing of the Red Sea, the escape from Egypt. The crux comes upon the mountain where God reveals to Moses the purpose of this salvation, the mountain where from the beginning God had said his people should serve him (Ex. 3.12). So in Ex. 19 and 20 the goal of the Exodus story is made clear. The Jews have been liberated in order that they may be partners to a covenant with God. They shall indeed be a nation within a nation, not to be the objects of oppression, but to be the agents of salvation. They shall be a holy nation within all the nations of the earth (Ex. 19.3–6).

22

Salvation, or liberation, is always a process which moves *from* a captivity into a freedom *for* a new quality and style of living. On the mountain Moses perceives an outline of what that style shall be. The children of Israel shall never again live under any other rule but the rule of God. In contrast to their slavery in Egypt, they are now free from bondage to any power save that of God alone.

Benjamin Uffenheimer of the University of Tel Aviv, Israel, writing about this Sinai covenant passage points out:

> The covenant with the divine king thus becomes the formative element in Israel's life. Against the background of Israel's experience in the house of slavery, the Kingdom of God seems to be Israel's antithesis defying any form of human bondage. In the course of Israel's history this concept developed into antagonism against any kind of human kingship. Monotheism was not born as an abstract philosophical system but as the theo-political response to human tyranny aiming at the creation of a unique framework for the life of Israel where every sphere of life is shaped by the exclusive will of the divine king. The realization of divine kingship in life – this is the real aim of Israel's liberation from bondage and of her entry into the promised land.[1]

The commandments that follow draw the guidelines of the new style of living, one in which men shall be free *from* any other claims to absolute sovereignty over their lives, so that God's exclusive rule, his holy name, his worship must be safeguarded, and one in which they shall be free *for* life in community, where property and personhood and respect for life are preserved by mutually agreed conventions of morality, in what is in effect a charter of human rights in a free society. Salvation from inhumane oppression culminates in a community where human values are given divine sanction.

The celebration of the Lord's liberation of the oppressed and of his covenant relationship with the law-abiding community is a frequent theme of the Psalms. Here is celebrated not solely the story of the salvation of the nation. Individual men and women have their own histories, set as they are in the context of the community's experience and worship. In the psalms we hear the celebration of many personal stories of salvation. Take, for example, Ps. 30, a prayer of thanksgiving for an experience which has been like a deliverance from death itself. No details are given about the experience. Like so many of these personal psalms it could be a description of almost any deep crisis in a person's life – a severe illness, an attack of depression, a loss of faith, a let-down by friends, an assault by enemies, a fall into temptation, a sudden bereavement. Whatever the experience, it is out of the depths of his own soul that the psalmist has cried out for salvation. It is the cry of a man alone with his own misery, facing a meaningless death. The most terrifying feature of human despair is this sense of isolation and meaninglessness. And his salvation comes, not simply as the healing of the sickness, though that is one part of the process, nor as mercy and comfort, though these too are attributes of God which he praises, but primarily on the restoration of new life, life lived in the presence of God and in the company of his people, life that is meaningful, life that not even death can destroy. It is even, the psalmist suggests, in the interest of God that he should be thus restored. God will be the loser if he is not saved. For his sense of isolation from God and of the meaninglessness of life is a denial of that covenant relationship to which God has committed himself, and in which all his people are caught up together to fulfil his purposes.

That same sense of personal isolation from God is the haunting theme of the psalm which was on our Lord's lips in the last moments on the cross, Ps. 22. It begins with the bewildered cry of every tormented human soul, 'My God, why?' There is no answer to this enigma of the apparent absence and silence of God at the time of acutest personal suffering. For the psalmist, the only way of encompassing this terrible loneliness is to recall the faith of his fathers, the faith he has himself imbibed with his mother's milk. To live without that faith would be like a denial of his own inheritance and identity. God may seem absent from the individual, but he dwells in the midst of the community which has praised him in the past and continues to praise him in the present, so the cry of an alienated sufferer, 'Why art thou far

24

from me?' turns to the plea of an anguished son, 'Be not far from me.'

The theme of this opening part of the psalm finds a haunting echo in a modern pop song of two singers who express poignantly the sense of God-forsakeness of so many of the present generation. Simon and Garfunkel's mocking cry 'Blessed' is a commentary on the conflict between the traditional truths they have been taught in their religious upbringing and the actual experience they endure in contemporary society.

Religion and drugs, both alike, seem escapes from the reality and pain of existence and the hell of the young singers is 'I've got no place to go . . .'

But the psalmist does have some place to go in search of his salvation. In v. 22 the complaint turns to confidence as he declares that in the midst of the congregation he will praise the faithfulness of God. For in that company, his immediate dilemma is set in the context of past and future, his personal situation seen in the perspective of God's dealings with all the sons of Israel, and all the nations of the earth. It is the community experience and the cosmic extent of salvation which become the theme of his song. In the midst of personal agony he acclaims the universal victory of God's kingdom; his own story is part of the total story of salvation. He is involved in all mankind. So he must pass on to another generation not the sense of the absence of God in his personal experience but faith in his presence throbbing through tribal memory and abiding with men in all ages to the end of time. This is not to escape suffering, but to transcend it, not to deny his personal identity but to fulfil it. The individual is saved *from* pre-occupation with his own dilemma as he joins the praises of the community; he is saved *for* commitment to coming generations as he takes up the theme of celebrating not his own experience but the mighty acts of God.

We thus see how in biblical songs of salvation, the individual and community are so inextricably linked together that one can never say of any psalm, 'this is purely personal', or 'this is a wholly corporate expression'. Salvation, even that which comes out of the depths of some personal experience, always has social consequences. It leads into community and commitment.

The social implications of salvation find their fullest expression in the writings of the prophets. In contrast to the complaints of personal sufferers, the target here is frequently the complacency of a whole nation, a people who have come to trust so completely in their salvation as the chosen ones of God that they have lost all awareness of what they are saved for. They have forgotten that the privilege of salvation brings with it the threat of judgment. 'The day of the Lord' can be one of darkness rather than light. For if salvation means the restoration of that relationship with God which renews the whole of human life, one manifestation of it should be that the life of God's people would reflect the consistency of God's own nature. He is a God of righteousness, of justice, whose cry to his people thunders through his prophet Amos:

> Let justice roll down like waters,
> and righteousness like an overflowing stream.

It is no wonder that the prophet Amos speaks so compellingly to the angry young people of today. So many of the things he cares deeply about, they care about too. In 1970 at a youth service in the Royal Albert Hall, groups of young protesters invaded the congregation and paraded through the arena the posters that are familiar now in most public demonstrations: 'Justice not Charity for the Poor'; 'How the Other Half Lives'; 'House Britain's Homeless'; 'Black Equals White'. Hunger, poverty, homelessness, racial injustice, the haunting nightmares of contemporary society, were placarded before us. Then leapt on to the stage a long-haired, bearded, hippie-type figure, clad in rough animal skin, and shouting to the protesters words like this:

> Come to the city and rebel – show them the injustice.
> They are the ones who are privileged and affluent,
> and therefore their responsibility is all the greater.
> So I will destroy their splendid houses,
> and take away their wealth,

26

and let them know what it feels like to be hungry.
Let them seek good and not evil,
that they may live.
Hate evil and love good,
and establish justice in the gate;
and maybe there is still a chance that the nation will be
    saved.

Only at that point did people begin to realize that this was a paraphrased Bible reading. It had such a contemporary ring about it that some even thought it had been specially written for the occasion. It raised right at the beginning of the service of worship the question of what worship is for, if it is not making people more alert to the word of God, a word of salvation and a word of judgment. The establishment of justice is not the means of salvation, but the effect of it; and where that effect is not apparent, then the claim to being partners of salvation must also be called in question. The credibility of the whole covenant relationship is imperilled when one partner clearly distorts the other's purposes for a just and humane society (Amos 3.2–3).

In the midst of ease and idleness, therefore, Amos prophesies doom. There will come soon a famine in the land, not of bread or water but of hearing the word of the Lord (Amos 8–11). The symptoms of this spiritual famine will be comparable to those of a physical one – the young will be restless and agitated, seeking desperately for some morsel of nourishment; older people, becoming accustomed to hunger, will sink into the paralysis of apathy, and finally perish in the poison of apostasy. Yet even so God will remain faithful to his promise. Out of dire destruction he will finally save his people. The sign of that salvation shall be the rebuilding of ruined cities, the replanting of devastated crops, the restoration of their homeland (Amos 9.13–15). The sin-shattered society shall be made whole again.

In days of affluence, the message of salvation comes as judgment. In days of suffering, it comes as comfort. To the exiles upon whom the doom has fallen a new prophet begins his message with the clear words 'Comfort ye, Comfort ye'. The promise of salvation is for them the promise of liberation from their captivity. That liberation is primarily a political one, the right to return to and to rebuild their own nation. As Samuel Amirtham points out:

Socially and economically the exiles did enjoy a certain amount of freedom. They were free to own property, to carry on business, and to meet for assemblies and worship. But they were longing for political freedom, freedom to return to their land and to the temple of their God. In 539, Cyrus rose to power in Persia and defeated the neo-Babylonian empire. The Jewish exiles were watching the turn of events with great interest, as did the rest of the world. There arose a great prophet among them who set himself to interpret the historical events and encourage a disheartened people by proclaiming the message of liberation (Isa. 40.1f.).[2]

This prophet of the exile points to two agents of God's salvation of his people. The one is a powerful political figure who, in spite of and unknown to himself, by his secular actions forwards the victory of God's cause. The other is a powerless, suffering man who, in total commitment to the will of God, by his life of perfect obedience becomes the sign of God's grace. Both are equally significant in the story. There is no suggestion that the one is more in accord with God's purposes than the other.

The beneficent political ruler, Cyrus, who in military victory defeats the oppressors of the Jewish people and allows the exiles to return home is even given the Davidic title 'Messiah', 'the anointed', an astonishing claim to make on behalf of a foreign king. His victory is attributed to the power of God working within him even without his acknowledgment. Indeed, Cyrus himself attributes his victory to his own God Marduk who led him by the hand and proclaimed him to be ruler of all the world and set him on the road to Babylon like a 'real friend'. Yet the prophet claims him as Yahweh's agent. He is the only God, his glory cannot be given to any other. The history of mankind is his story. The victory of Cyrus is his vindication.

Samuel Amirtham in his commentary on this passage makes an interesting comparison between Cyrus and the modern leaders of independence and liberation movements.

All who fight for human liberation, dignity and justice, he suggests, are God's agents. He refers to a contemporary Hindu poet, Bharathiar, who expresses his view of salvation in the following terms which have parallels in the vision of the prophet of the exile:

> Will man habitually be robbing man of his food any more?
> Will he keep watching another's agony (in silence)?
> Sweet rivers, long fields has our land in plenty,
> Fruits and roots and corn in abundance shall be evermore.
> We will make a new law and protect it,
> We will destroy the whole world if food be lacking for one.
> Every being is 'I am', said Lord Krishna.
> Divine status for every man shall be
> India's gift to the world.

All of one caste	All of same cost
All of one race	All of same price
All are Indians	All shall be Kings, Kings of this land.

The same poet has written a poem about Mahatma Gandhi. It is a dialogue with God in which Gandhi asks God what he is going to do to relieve the oppression of the people of India. God answers him saying that he will send and use Gandhi. Can we as Christians as boldly as the Jewish prophet claim Mahatma Gandhi as an agent of God's salvation? 'The church is called', concludes Samuel Amirtham, 'to discern in faith God's agents in world history and proclaim them to the world. Some may ask; Is not identifying unknown agents of God a cheap theological game? How can we, in doing so, remain faithful to God's revelation in Christ? How can we also be true to the integrity and self-understanding of such agents? And yet is it not an imperative laid on us who stand in Deutero-Isaiah's tradition, and who worship his God, the Lord of history?[3]

The other agent is no great ruler but a slave bound to obedience to his master's service. He performs no public role; he exercises no kingly right (Isa. 42.2f.). Yet quietly, gently, graciously he pursues the cause of justice, reminding the people of God's just claims upon them and of their rights and responsibilities towards one another. He is not discouraged by the difficulty and long delay in the fulfilment of his task. He waits and works on patiently confident in the covenant God has made with him and with his people. God's faithfulness and the servant's consistency will be a sign to all the world of what that covenant relationship means. He will open the eyes of the blind, release those who are imprisoned, illumine those who sit in darkness (Isa. 42.7). He will become the symbol of light, liberty, life for all mankind. But he will not immediately be acclaimed. Rather than being hailed as the agent of God's salvation he will be scorned as the evidence of failure (Isa. 53). His powerlessness, his passion will make him an object of derision. Yet he will remain faithful. Being one of the oppressed himself he bears upon his body the very marks of their suffering. Yet in that suffering he is saved – kept faithful to the covenant, an obedient servant.

The identity of this suffering servant remains the prophet's secret. Unlike Cyrus, the political liberator, he is nameless. He may be a representative figure, through which the prophet depicts the role of the people of Israel. To the Christian he is a pre-figuring of Jesus who chose the way of the suffering servant as the way of salvation.

In today's world the church is called to be just such an obedient, patient, powerless servant of the consistency of God's love and the commandments of his justice. This does not deny the realities of the political struggle, nor the effectiveness of power that is used responsibly. But it remains a witness to a salvation that lies beyond the power game, to a liberation that can loosen the bonds of oppressed and oppressor alike and set all men free for that open, loving, just relationship with God and with one another which is the new thing God offers to all mankind.

Just as the agents of salvation are twofold, so too are the aspects of salvation presented by the prophet. Not only does salvation mean liberation, it also means forgiveness (Isa. 44.22). Not only does it reach out to Israel, it reaches the ends of the earth (Isa. 45.22). Not only does it keep a continuity with the past, the return of the exiles being frequently reminiscent of the Exodus from Egypt, it is also a break with that past, the ushering in of a new age (Isa. 43.18f.). The very real continuity is the consistency between what God says and what he does. The history of the people of Israel has vindicated the covenant. The future of the people of God will likewise witness to his faithfulness. Through many agencies, public and secret, political and spiritual, powerful and powerless, victorious and suffering, through unwitting instruments and committed servants, God's purpose will be fulfilled and all the ends of the earth shall see his salvation.

4

Today's Announcement

Salvation as Good News Now

'Today this scripture has been fulfilled in your hearing'
(Luke 4.21). With this splendid announcement Jesus began
his preaching in Nazareth. No wonder the congregation
hung upon the preacher's words to see what he would say
next. He had chosen to expound what must have been one
of their favourite passages from the prophets, that promise
of liberation which had kept hope alive through the dark
days of exile, that had sustained the chosen people through
the long haul back to the Promised Land and that now in
these latest days of Roman occupation and oppression held
out new promise of a coming Messiah. The congregation in
the synagogue listened with rapt attention as Jesus read the
sacred words.

Then suddenly the mood changed. It was the exposition
that enraged them. In his sermon Jesus did three things that
the congregation found intolerable. First, he placed the
prophetic message firmly in a contemporary context – today.
This salvation was to be seen not simply as a future hope,
nor as a past glory, but to be discerned close at hand as a
present reality. Secondly, he related it to actual happenings
locally, what had been going on in their own land, not
singling it out for any special glory but rather for particular
blame. Thirdly, he gave the whole message a universal

significance, attributing to the land of Sidon and even to the foreigner Naaman an experience of salvation which the people of Israel had believed to be their exclusive privilege. This really was going too far and the congregation could stand no more of it. The preacher brought down upon his head not simply the wrath of political authorities who might have detected within his proclamation echoes of the contemporary rebelliousness of an oppressed people, nor that of religious leaders who could hardly believe that any good thing could come from a mere layman of Nazareth, but even of his own company. They were outraged when they discovered that he identified himself not with the protection of their privilege and the preservation of their tradition as the chosen people but with the undiscriminating offer of salvation to all mankind. Such a concept of salvation today was too disturbing to be tolerated, the preacher was never allowed to complete his sermon.

The scandal of such contemporary preaching today, as then, is the radical contradiction between the good news being proclaimed and the evil world people experience. It is all right for a preacher to recall the salvation of yesterday or to promise salvation tomorrow, but in all honesty how could anyone claim to see evidence of salvation today? Unless the preacher could produce miracles to prove what he said, who could be expected to take him seriously? Later in his ministry, Jesus did indeed point to tangible evidence of the salvation he preached. In answer to a question about his credentials as the divine messenger he said, 'Go and tell John what you have seen and heard: the blind receive their sight, the lame walk, lepers are cleansed, and the deaf hear, the dead are raised up, the poor have good news preached to them. And blessed is he who takes no offense at me' (Luke 7.22f.). All these signs of compassion illustrate God's undiscriminating love, reaching to the lowliest, the most needy, the most powerless. Most remarkable of all is the way this love reaches the least deserving, the sinners, the outcasts, even the exploiters, because this Saviour can forgive sin and restore right relationships. So even Zacchaeus whose exploitation of his fellowmen had led to his total isolation found himself accepted by Jesus, and through that acceptance discovered the grace to put right the wrongs he had done and was then restored to the human community: 'Today salvation has come to this house' (Luke 19.1–10). Where disgrace brings isolation grace brings acceptance.

Today the proclamation of the good news becomes credible only when it is accompanied by acts of compassion and by signs of grace. The good news has to be made evident in each particular situation as something that is close at hand to be discerned and revealed by those who can see where and how God's grace is at work. This calls for a new look at each situation in the light of the gospel of love. Jesus illustrates this new look by the unexpected twists in the stories he tells to illustrate what the Kingdom of God is like. It is like the home of a loving father welcoming back a penitent son, but the twist comes when we discover that it is not only the obvious sinner who needs the salvation of his father's love, but also the apparently upright hard-working loyal son who has never learned to love either his father or his brother and therefore is incapable of celebrating the forgiveness of sin and the reconciliation of the family (Luke 15.11f.). Again it is expressed through the action of a foreigner who refuses to allow barriers of prejudice to prevent him from crossing the road to show compassion to a fellowman and who thereby becomes unwittingly the bearer of a gospel which must break down all barriers of race or status or circumstance (Luke 10.30–37). To look for the gospel in any situation is to look for that which today restores relationship, forgives sin, celebrates love, enacts compassion.

On the occasion of the twenty-fifth anniversary of the World Council of Churches, the General Secretary, Dr Philip Potter, chose as his text the sermon of Jesus at Nazareth and commenting on the significance of the word *today* said:

> Our own today is that there is bad news for the poor all over the world – they are getting poorer. Those who are oppressed in today's world have little or no hope of liberation. Those who are morally or spiritually blind seem to have no prospect of seeing. There is no sign of God's purpose being fulfilled. Jesus, on the

contrary, invites us to make real his 'Today' . . . Here is the authentic Today – the moment of vision of God's will to free all men and women from whatever binds them, towards fullness of life and for each other . . .

It is therefore biblically right and proper that the World Council and its member churches should be concerned about poverty, oppression, blindness and despair everywhere. In Jesus' ministry he was very specific in fulfilling the message of the Kingdom. The hungry in body and spirit, the sick, the demon-possessed, the outcast prostitutes and profiteers, were the subjects of this 'Today' of God's liberating power and grace. And the price of his 'Today' was the cross. We who continue his ministry dare not do less, and more we cannot do.[1]

The consistency of love which characterized Jesus' whole ministry is consummated on the cross, the clearest demonstration that the gospel is not about the security of the faithful or the power of the righteous but about invincible love for all mankind. This is a love which refuses to transmit to others the effects of man's enmity, suspicion, jealousy. It absorbs all this sin into itself, even to the point of paying the full penalty, the wages of sin, which is death. It is a love which dare risk everything and lays aside all its power. It is this love, says Jesus, which will draw all men unto him. It is this love which *today* can promise paradise to a penitent thief. It is this love which is the seal of the new covenant which Christians will celebrate whenever they eat together of the bread and drink of the cup which proclaims his death. It is this love which will release men from their fears and their sins for a new relationship with God and with their fellow men which, like the old covenant, is expressed in an obedience to his new commandment that they love one another even as he has loved them (I John 4.7–21).

The vindication of this love is the resurrection of Jesus from the dead. Here is the final evidence that nothing, not even the might of death itself, can destroy love. So it is faith in the resurrection which gives people confidence to face the cost of loving right through to the bitter end. The death of self, which is the inevitable ultimate expression of love, would be impossible to face without the faith that beyond such death lies the certainty of new life.

35

If this is to be a saving faith, it needs to be related to the reality of the situations in which people live in contemporary society. An industrial chaplain speaking once of the deadlock so often experienced in industrial relations, where neither management nor union dare face the defeat of any of the interests they are commissioned to defend, said, 'I find the only thing that can save in a situation like this is when someone has enough faith to risk letting go his own interests and thus releases a new element in the situation – in other words, the courage to face death in order that resurrection might happen.' The same is true of a breakdown in human relationship, personal or political. Salvation comes only through that quality of loving which dare face, and even absorb, defeat and hate and loss and death in the belief that ultimately love is vindicated and new life breaks through.

So the resurrection of Jesus gives people courage to proclaim and to enact the salvation of which he is the Author and the Name. Throughout the Book of Acts this salvation becomes the theme of the apostles – 'there is no other name under heaven given among men by which we must be saved' (Acts 4.12). There is no other way than that which Jesus has demonstrated and which they in the power of the spirit poured out upon them express in their own words and deeds. It is essential that everyone shall get the message. So the apostles are enabled to speak in tongues which everyone can understand. They break through all the usual barriers to communication that prevent human beings from hearing one another. They bridge the generation gap as the spirit prompts old men to dream dreams and young men to see visions; they ignore sex discrimination as sons and daughters both together are inspired to prophesy. They even break down the human Babel of different languages and cultures as everyone hears in his own language the mighty works of God (Acts 2). The meaning of their message is demonstrated by their acts. They show compassion to a crippled man, they confront the authorities, they develop a new kind of community life in commitment to one another. As a result there is added to their number daily those who are being saved and who then become caught up in this new saving community of men and women living in the power of the spirit.

Surely we see that same spirit breaking through in our society today. Wherever a man has a dream of what human community could be and backs that dream with his life; wherever men and women protest against all that dehumanizes or discriminates; wherever people reach out to each other across the barriers of race and culture and creed, there opens up the way of salvation. Wherever people commit themselves to one another in a community of caring and compassion, wherever folk celebrate life and affirm love, wherever hope is kindled and faith kept alive and love is unlimited, there is glimpsed the joy of salvation.

This spirit-filled, saving community is but a foretaste of what all human community would be like in the new age of which Paul writes in such confident expectation in his great letter about salvation, the letter to the Romans (Rom. 8.18ff.). Here Paul, recognizing how helpless the contemporary human situation is, writes of the rescue which will come from outside when God, the great Judge, will set men free from all that enslaves them, so that they might enjoy the glorious liberty that is the true heritage of his son. He will put right all that has gone wrong in perverted relationships. He will reconcile the whole world to himself when he and all mankind will see that the full penalty of all man's sin has been paid in the redeeming and saving love of Jesus. Summing up the human situation as Paul depicts it, Kenneth Grayston writes:

> Human beings live a distorted existence which God's salvation aims at removing and putting right. We behave as aliens and enemies, we lack security, and we perversely misuse the rules by which men could live. We are in fact enslaved, so that our actions are marked by wickedness and decay. For this to be put right we need to be set free – that is, to be reconciled, to establish new relationships and take up new responsibilities, to share the glory and the sonship of God. [2]

Accepting the reality of the fact that in their present condition all men and women seem to be enslaved to the twin tyrants of sin and death and under compulsion to use their bodily powers to carry out the tyrants' plan, Paul sees salvation as a release from this slavery and an enrolment in God's service, using our bodily powers to promote what is good (Rom. 6.12f.). The only way the transition from slavery to freedom can be made, however, is by death, by 'dying to sin' (ceasing to live in a situation controlled by sin) and 'living to God' (living in a situation controlled by God). This has been done by Jesus (Rom. 6.9f.) and can be done by all who identify themselves with his death and become committed to the new life in a situation controlled by God.

Kenneth Grayston warns us against giving too personal and individual an interpretation to this concept. When Paul writes 'we know that our old self was crucified with him so that the sinful body might be destroyed and we might no longer be enslaved to sin', the word translated 'self' is *anthropos* which can be rendered 'human existence', and the words 'sinful body' could be expressed by 'corporate sinfulness'. 'So', writes Grayston, 'we can conclude that baptismal identification with the death of Christ is not simply (though it may include) an individual experience and conversation, but the destruction of a human existence dominated by sinful activity and the creation of a new existence dominated by God.'[3]

All this, however, is but an interim experience of a salvation, the full glory of which is still to be realized. Paul writes of salvation always as a looking forward, an anticipation of a totally new order. Usually he uses the verb 'to be saved' in the future tense and even when uncharacteristically he uses a past tense (Rom. 8.24) he immediately links it with the idea of hope, in the sense of confident expectation of that which still has to be fully experienced. Final salvation belongs to the future, beyond the events that will conclude the human story and restore the kingdoms of this world to their rightful Ruler. Before then there will be more intense suffering, more oppressive subjection to evil powers, but then Christ will return to claim his own Kingdom, to carry out the final judgment and to inaugurate the new order. Already these coming events have cast their shadows before in the suffering, death and resurrection of Jesus. Those who place their trust in him can claim with confidence the mercy that will carry them safely through the judgment and can live as though they already share in the glorious liberty of the new age. In that new age the whole of creation will be rescued from its present chaos and restored to the order which is God's design for it (Rom. 8.19–22).

Thus while recognizing with sober realism, even pessimism, the futility and decay of the present state of affairs, Paul sees the world always still as God's world, an arena where hope is possible and where God co-operates with men for good (Rom. 8.28). The very protesting cries and turmoil of the present age are evidence of some possibility beyond its enslavement. As Grayston puts it:

> Indeed, the liberation experienced by the people of God is to be extended to the created world. When God's children experience the glory of the new age, the world itself will be transformed with them and for them . . . [God's] final purpose and his forward planning has designated his Son as the only available model of humanity in the new age. God alone decides that destiny, invites men to accept it, removes their present distortion and gives them the expected glory.[4]

The last word as the first is with God. Without him mankind is helpless. With him human beings become the agents of salvation living as those who, in face of decay and impending destruction, by faith in Christ live in active anticipation of the new order. Already the people of faith experience the liberation which will be the heritage of all men when all things shall be restored and the whole human community be reconciled to God. That experience can begin now. Today, says Paul, is the day of salvation (I Cor. 6.2)

5

Meeting at Bangkok

Reflections on the Conference on 'Salvation Today'

'Salvation! Where can I find salvation?' screamed the young Japanese artist as he raced through the dining hall of the Red Cross Centre a few miles from Bangkok on a hot January day. The three hundred people busy over their lunch paused and smiled appreciatively at this latest attempt to dramatize the theme of their Conference. 'Yet another "happening" laid on by an imaginative Asian,' they registered mentally, 'all good modern conference technique. Makes a pleasant change from speeches.' And they turned back to their soup. Then suddenly there was a frenzied cry, a splash and a wild flaying of arms. The young man had thrown himself into the pool outside the hall where deep waters had engulfed him. His shouts for someone to save him brought doctors and Red Cross helpers hurrying to the scene. This was no role-play. This was for real. A man was drowning. No time for words now, only for action.

The incident remains vividly in the memory for it was an acted parable of the whole life of the extraordinary Conference on Salvation Today held under the auspices of the World Council of Churches in Thailand at the beginning of 1973. Three hundred and twenty-six people from fifty-nine countries came together for ten days to seek new meaning in this old word of faith, salvation. The setting was Asia and the largest group of participants were from Asia, Africa and Latin America. So for once Asian styles of communication broke through our usual Western worlds of words, and in cartoon, drama, visual display and majestic Thai dancing, meaning was expressed that so often eludes our attempts to verbalize everything.

Most memorable were the contributions of Yushi, the Japanese artist, whose anguish over the theme so nearly led him to personal tragedy and who daily prodded the Conference through his cartoons to see themselves as a comedy, playing games with words in the midst of human despair. Could Jesus drag this waggon-load of slogan-shouting Christians right into the agonies of the real world he had come to save? Would the heavenly bodies of the ecumenical jet-set ever really come down to earth? (See the cartoons at the beginning of this book.) Half way through the Conference, on the floor of the appropriately named Happy Hall where the plenary sessions were held, among all the litter of amended documents and abandoned resolutions lay significantly a Japanese paper-made crucifix easily trampled over by those who passed by, hurrying on to the next verbal battle, oblivious of the crucified One lying at their feet.

Scepticism about the choice of the theme came from many quarters before the Conference was held. Some thought it unnecessary to debate such a fundamental word of the faith, while others thought it meaningless to concentrate on so religious a theme. Some were afraid that the concept of salvation would be diluted for the sake of ecumenical dialogue; others thought it would be a hindrance to the growing dialogue with other faiths. Some thought this marked a retreat from the secular understanding of mission, others welcomed the opportunity of theologically undergirding contemporary concerns. Some expected the theme to emphasize personal, spiritual, private experience; others hoped it would concentrate on political, material, public issues.

In the event most of the hopes were realized and few of the fears justified. One of the official Conference reflectors confessed that he came with feelings of ambivalence, partly because he felt that in the preparatory materials the conservative evangelical position to which he was committed seemed to be relegated to the small print, and partly because he was preoccupied with problems related to his own work at home. Reflecting on the Conference at the end he wrote:

The Conference was not what I had expected. Whereas I experienced perplexity and sadness, I also was surprised, and could not but rejoice. Now that the Conference is over, the following 'signs of salvation' appear significant:

1. We were willing to grapple fairly with many biblical categories related to Salvation Today. Our only regret was that we could not also explore such crucial themes as the righteous wrath of God and the work of the Holy Spirit.

2. We were conscious that we cannot speak of *salvation and social justice* without reaffirming a biblical and theological base that is distinctly Christian.

3. We represented considerable diversity in our understanding and performance of the task of Christian mission. If we accept this diversity and seek to express our unity in Christ, the gospel of reconciliation will be proclaimed to this generation and social justice will be furthered in the earth. However, only by exercising a pastoral care for one another can this total task be accomplished.

I sense a personal obligation to probe more deeply into the biblical implications of the Christian role of *herald* and *servant* and of the *cross* that displays the powerlessness and power of God.[1]

Echoing these words was the testimony of another reflector at the other end of the theological spectrum, a man intensely involved in social action and the struggle for economic justice in the world. He wrote of his experience at Bangkok:

At times I experienced no other common bond and underpinning except the naked commitment to support and care for one another, and that seemed enough for does not Salvation Today for me start there?

I worry at the understandable priority among so many, given to political and economic liberation, as if once so liberated, we are truly free – open to others, willing to take the risk of love, of trust; – open to our whole selves, our lives of intuition as well as logic, of contemplation as well as action, of solitude as well as company; no longer enslaved to the manipulation of others, to the arrogant use of our creative powers . . .

I suspect God has far less hang-ups with us than we have, and so he sustains us in good humour – an aspect of Christian hope. I felt little profound humour the first seven days here, maybe because we weren't taking ourselves seriously enough.

I suspect God, who knows us struggling Christians better than we understand ourselves, is far less frustrated than I am with 'the less than complete' or 'lack of a perfect success' at our meeting. In that bewildering thought, captured only in faith, I rejoice at what we have done here.[2]

Perplexity and joy, diversity and unity, social concern and personal caring, humour and openness – all these were shared experiences at Bangkok through which we learned more about the meaning of salvation than any academic exposition could have given us. The Conference itself had a wholeness about it in the wide range of its programme and the variety of its constituency that reflected the comprehensiveness of the theme we had come to study. We had been told that the first purpose of the meeting at Bangkok was to celebrate and proclaim the richness of salvation as a gift of God through the Holy Spirit, as witnessed to by the scriptures, and as experienced by men and women today in their struggle for meaning and fullness of life and for social justice.

We certainly did celebrate. In ways ancient and modern, Eastern and Western, sacred and secular we shared together the joy of our salvation. With American saxophones and African drums, in Orthodox chant and Pentecostal choruses, in folk songs and pop music, we made a joyful noise to the Lord, making up in enthusiasm what we lacked in harmony, and that in itself was a good ecumenical parable. We even broke out on occasion into dancing, each at first doing our own thing but ending in a kind of great ecumenical hokey-cokey which seems to belong to all cultures. We learned to laugh at and with one another as we shared each other's jokes and folk lore. (Incidentally the British delegates found themselves as usual at a loss when invited to contribute at a barbecue concert something typical of their own culture, and finally fell back on what was introduced as 'a dance of one of our hill tribes in the north, the Gay Gordons'!)

We saw the old year out in a splendid performance of classical Thai dancing followed by a watchnight service in which we shared with our neighbours our hopes and fears for the coming year. We sang Auld Lang Syne in the sultry heat of a Bangkok night with candles lighting up the black and brown and yellow and white faces of the new acquaintances who would now never be forgotten. We drank the cup of kindness together, the cup of the new covenant which makes us all kinsfolk. And all this seemed a foretaste of the festivities of heaven. In the end, salvation is something to sing about.

We shared the witness of the scriptures and our personal experiences of salvation in small study groups which achieved in the first three days an astonishing depth of intimacy between people from widely different backgrounds. The majority of the groups concentrated on biblical texts. Indeed so many participants opted for Bible study that three extra groups had to be formed. But others reached deep levels of understanding too as they considered salvation in relation to meditation, to music, to the arts, to health and healing, to suffering, ill-health and death. Though none of these groups were pressed to make reports, most of us were so enriched by the group experience that we felt we just had to find ways of sharing it with the Conference. Indeed the very process of communicating with others became a factor in our community life.

Participation was a key feature of the Conference and the small groups, and later the large sections, into which the Conference divided made this more possible than usual at large gatherings. Even in the plenary sessions of Bible study under the skilled leadership of Hans-Ruedi Weber, the Conference became a buzz of working minds and voices rather than an audience. Yet there were moments too of deep silence – a shared contemplation of a mystery that spoke to all of us as we read together the psalmist crying out his sense of forsakeness, as we looked at artists' attempts to express the agony of the crucifixion and realized again the

44

centrality of suffering, as we listened to music trumpeting the triumph of the risen and ascended Lord.

So we came together in worship. Emilio Castro writing in the *International Review of Missions* described the worship thus: 'The secret heart of the life of the Conference beat in the worship service celebrated every day at noon in which everybody was invited to express himself in his own language. This service of prayer and adoration was the occasion for bringing all the disagreements, anxieties, and hope of the community into the presence of God.'[3]

The cry 'Out of the depths I cry unto thee O Lord' was the haunting refrain of all our intercessions uttered as they were out of a multiplicity of agonizing situations of oppression, conflict, perplexity and despair. Even the experience of being at the Conference itself brought its own agony of sense of helplessness. We were meeting in Thailand in January 1973 and even as we met to debate the meaning of salvation we could almost hear the roar of the American B52 bombers taking off from their bases nearby to unleash hell on North Vietnam in the name of the salvation of Western civilization. But what could we do about it? Were we utterly powerless? One of the participants thought not. R. J. van der Veen, Secretary of the Dutch Missionary Society, galvanized the Conference when he said in the first Open Hearing:

> I went to four services over Christmas. In all four services I heard a despairing pastor trying to talk about the Christmas message of peace with the brutal at-random bombing in North Vietnam going on. We are here just an hour's flight away from North Vietnam. The planes leave from this country in order to carry their death-bringing load to the east. I want to submit to the Conference a suggestion how we as Christians can do something about this murdering. If a hundred of us went to Hanoi, if we informed the American President that we were going and that we would put our bodies between American bombs and the people of North Vietnam, that would be a 'reasonable service'.

Was it reasonable or was it madness? The debate raged on for days and with each session despair intensified. Surely salvation could not be as simple as all that! People going out to lay down their lives? Yet that sounded uncomfortably like what it is all about. Most of us knew deep down we had neither the courage nor the conviction to face it and we felt helpless to know what else to do. We delayed decision by debate and avoided commitment by referring the whole matter to another committee. So the servant church did nothing except pass a strong recommendation condemning the war, and left the political leaders to get on with the peace negotiations.

One phrase from the Vietnam resolution expressed a theme that came through very strongly throughout the Conference. Out of our sense of helplessness we were yet able to testify: 'Even when we are powerless and our voice is ignored we must remember that we act out of obedience and not only because of our expectation to win.' The whole question of power in relation to the church and its mission of salvation recurred constantly in debates between the so-called 'third world' and the West. This was one of the most marked features of the Bangkok Conference. There was on the one hand the recognition that power exercised responsibly can save. The history of salvation is the history of God's exercise of power to set men free. The power of God penetrates the political, economic and cultural structures of mankind and also invades the intimacy of man's heart.

Yet, on the other hand, we were all too tragically aware at Bangkok that it is power that oppresses, that causes suffering, that kills. Rubem Alves of Latin America writes in his reflections on Bangkok:

The irony of power is not that it destroys when it is consciously used for the purpose of destruction, but rather that most of the time, in history, the best of men's intentions produce the most inhuman results. It seems that power has a corrupting effect so that that which seemed, in the beginning, to be the power of the Christ, at the end reveals itself as demonic. The church, for one thing, has been a sad spectacle of this tragedy . . .

One of the sources of inspiration and enthusiasm of the missionary movement was the optimistic identification of God's power with Western power . . . The West always considered its

46

civilization as the social and historical expression of the Hebraic and Christian tradition. This is the reason, it was argued, why the West makes history, whereas the non-western cultures are a-historical. If this was the case, conversion to Christ had to imply the abdication of one's culture and of one's peculiar way of life ·. . .

The passive acceptance of this state of affairs, however, is over. The Bangkok Conference was filled with both resentment and anger, on the part of those who were subjected to colonial–missionary domination, and guilt feelings on the part of those who sponsored the Western economic, political and ideological invasion of the third world. Once in a while one had the impression that this had become a sort of sado-masochist complex, whereby oppressed and oppressors resolved, by means of linguistic rituals, the hard realities of the master-slave relationship which characterized their common past. It seems to me that here we have a point on which all the participants agreed: unless the West ceases to dominate the third world, there is no possibility of salvation. But we do not have any clear ideas as to how to accomplish this goal. Because history does not know of any case in which oppressors have willingly given up power . . .

Power is needed to change the situation. But we are powerless. [Our powerlessness was never more poignantly felt than when we discussed Vietnam.] It is this contradiction which characterizes the apocalyptic situation. One sees the seeming omnipotence of the powers of evil. One looks for signs of an approaching liberation. But one finds nothing. Optimism is impossible. The available alternatives are either to join the dominant powers and to become fat with the flesh pots of Egypt, or else to go insane . . .

This, it seems to me, is the shape of the problem of salvation today. Both in domestication and in insanity, humanity is lost . . . The possibility of salvation is the possibility of communal life in which one is able to hope in a hopeless situation. According to the Bible it is possible to remain free and human even in captivity (Jer. 29). As someone put it: 'In the past we were sure that the church was the vanguard of a movement which would transfigure the world in our lifetime. We no longer believe it. The new question is: How can the church, in her powerlessness, be a supportive and healing community – the servant church – which will preserve human life human, till the right time comes?' Obviously salvation, at least in our time, cannot be equated with happiness. If one has eyes to see, one cannot be happy. Happiness is possible only by anticipation – as a result of that communal experience which reassures one that the value of love, forgiveness, mercy and freedom are not lost. And as these values become fresh in concrete communities, we may be sure that the Spirit is still at work.[4]

Yet the Conference newspaper was able to come out in its first edition with the bold headline *Happy are the people who are in such a state.* The sentence was taken from the first of only two major addresses at the Conference, a personal statement on the meaning of salvation given by M. M. Thomas, Director of the Christian Institute in Bangalore and Chairman of the WCC Central Committee. He chose as the theme of his address Ps. 144 and the prayer for the ideal society which is presented there. The psalmist's hopes, he suggested, are very much like the aspirations of the people of India today as they yearn for a richer and fuller human life. Vital elements to the well-being of society are health of body and beauty of form for young people, encouraged gladly to affirm their sexuality in both its romantic and erotic aspects. Then there is the desire for material abundance, for full barns and fat cattle. Alongside this is the longing for peace and security from aggression, no 'leading into captivity', 'no breaking in nor going out'. Fourthly the psalmist prays for social justice so that there may be 'no cries of distress in our public places'.

Health and plenty, peace and justice, these elements in the secular pursuit of happiness are the context in which one may speak of spiritual salvation as the psalmist himself does. For after picturing the society of his dreams he says:

> Happy the people to whom such blessings fall!
> Happy the people whose God is the Lord!

Thus in this main address M. M. Thomas grasped firmly the nettle of controversy as to whether salvation is a spiritual or a material concept, whether it has personal or political implications. He did so by defining what is meant by 'spirituality'. Spirituality, he declared, is the true mark of humanity, it is that which distinguishes man from animals. Man belongs to the animal species and yet at the same time has a self-awareness which enables him even when involved in natural processes to transcend them. By responsible choice he gives to the processes themselves a spiritual quality of meaning and sacredness. For example, the sex act is for human beings never simply a physical process but a spiritual union between two people. Within the sacredness and inter-personal commitment of marriage, such a union can be means of personal fulfilment. Where there is no meaningful relationship such union can lead to personal disintegration. Similarly, the provision of food can be either a self-indulgence or a genuine recognition of need. 'Bread for myself is a material question', said Nicholas Berdyaev, 'Bread for my neighbour is a spiritual one.' So the problems of economics are shot through with human spiritualities as are all striv-ings for health and happiness, for development and justice. The only question is whether it is true or false spirituality, whether it is directed towards the ultimate meaning and sacredness which is God, or towards self-centredness and rejection of God which is idolatrous.

Mission is concerned therefore with the salvation of human spirituality and its direction towards that ultimate meaning and fulfilment of life which is revealed in the life, death and resurrection of Jesus. When all the strivings for a fuller human life are seen as means to witness to the God and Father of our Lord Jesus Christ as the only God worthy of men's worship, then indeed men and their aspirations are truly saved and made human, a foretaste of the ultimate offered by God in Christ to all mankind. So the mission of the church is to share in all these human strivings of both persons and societies in such a way as to reveal Jesus as the source, the judge and Redeemer of the human spirituality evident in all these movements of liberation.

This does not mean that there is no false spirituality active in the strivings of human society. M. M. Thomas mentioned a whole gamut of modern idols – hunger for power, affluence as the be all and end all, pollution, exploita-tion, revolutions which become themselves oppressive, secu-larism which becomes self-sufficient. 'This', he said, 'is the same old vicious circle of law, sin and death (Rom. 7) and we are today more conscious of its reality and its power than during any previous period.' He went on:

It is precisely at this point that the victory of the cross is relevant. The mission of the church in this context is to be present within the creative liberation movements of our time which the gospel of Christ itself has helped to take shape, and so to be able to communicate the genuine gospel of liberation – from the vicious circle of sin and alienation, law and self-righteousness, frustration and death into the new realm of Christ's New Humanity where there is forgiveness and recon-ciliation, grace and justification, renewal and eternal life. It is this message that will liberate the liberation movements from the false spiritual structures of meaning based on idolatrous worship of schemes of self-redemption, and thus redeem their creative impulses from self-destructive tendencies, enabling them to achieve their inner rationale of human emancipation. Our message of Christ's Salvation is ever the same; it is the call to men and nations to turn 'from idols to serve a living God' who has 'translated us from the domain of darkness into the Kingdom of his dear Son Jesus Christ.'[5]

In the light of so comprehensive a view of salvation and so clear a definition of spirituality the old Western debates about the relative importance of personal and social dimen-sions of salvation and about its spiritual and material mani-festations seemed sterile and meaningless. M. M. Thomas' emphasis had been on the salvation of the whole of human life, everything human – individuality and collectivity in-cluded, all of which have roots of different levels of self-awareness, sense of spiritual freedom and responsibility and the search for meaning and sacredness.

This was the context in which the rest of the Conference discussions went on. We divided then into three main sec-tions of our theme to look at questions of salvation and cul-ture and identity, salvation and social justice, salvation and churches renewed in mission. Through them all, Asian, African and Latin American voices kept insistently calling us back to this concept of the wholeness of our message. Refusing to be sidetracked into European academic theo-logical debates, voices from the third world thundered their emphasis that salvation must relate to the whole of life, to a man's personal identity and a people's political destiny, to a person's private sins and a nation's institutionalized guilt, to a child's cry for bread and a teenager's search for meaning. Somehow our ears must be opened to hear the many varied cries for salvation that are for real all round us.

6

Letting People Be

Salvation and Identity

'Let me be!' That frustrated cry of a teenager to her doting parents may sound at first like a plea to be left alone. Listen more carefully and you hear a deeper yearning, a cry for a love that can let go and let live, that no longer seeks to direct or even protect but is able to release the young adult into the full maturity of her selfhood.

To be or not to be is not a question of staying alive or committing suicide. It is the dilemma of trying to discover what one's real being is, what it means to be truly oneself. The search for a sense of identity, personal, national or racial, is a frequent theme of contemporary literature. In the anthology entitled *Salvation Today and Contemporary Experience* one of the most haunting passages is a transcript of a conversation recorded by Tony Parker with a girl selling ties in Oxford Street. Gradually she describes how she sees herself, first in terms of the facts of her existence, then how she feels about it, then her search for some whole identity, for salvation.

What am I? Well I'm just a girl who sells ties on the street, that's all. I live with my sister Tessa in a furnished room and we make the ties together. She goes to John Lewis's one week and buys some material and we cut them out and sew them up and then the next week it's my turn to go and choose it and we take it in turns like that. Sometimes I make a lot of money. One week before Christmas I made over fifty pounds. Another time it'll be raining and you hardly take anything at all. Now and again if I'm really broke I go to the National Assistance but not very often because I don't like doing it, it's degrading somehow: I think everyone should manage for themselves if they possibly can, but on the other hand I don't like living on Tessa's money either and rather than borrow from her I go there – mixed up you see as usual, aren't I? . . .

I did a sculpture once, a kind of self-portrait thing: just before I left the college. It was only an experiment: it didn't work out very well so I broke it up again. It was very funny, it had only one eye, in fact it was only half a face if you see what I mean, and the rest of it was one of my usual splodges. This part was very realistic, done very carefully with lots of detail and then the other side of it was all pushed back and out of shape. In a way it had a sort of shield effect. You know, the part that looked like my face was protecting the other part. Very symbolic, I suppose, half a face formed and the other half still out of shape and not certain what it was going to be.[1]

So articulate a street-trader would seem to be evidently a drop-out from the artificiality of the Western society which had nurtured her, given her a college training and turned her out into the world with no clear idea of her identity. The one thing she refused was the mask which convention had compelled her to wear. At least she would, in the words of so many contemporary youngsters, 'do her own thing'. Yet she seemed still uncertain of what her own thing was.

People with half faces usually wear masks. Sydney Carter in one of his songs tells a whole life-story through the masks a man wears – the mask of a baby, of a schoolboy, of a lover, of a soldier, of a married man. But this song ends with a triumphant finale:

> Ring the bell for a dead man
> Just bury the mask, that's all I ask
> Ring the bell for a dead man
> You'll never bury me.[2]

Salvation is the discovery in life as well as in death of that essential me that lies behind the mask, the restoration of that whole face that has been so marred, even in the hands of the sculptor.

Sometimes one does meet a 'saved person' who bears about in herself a quality of being wholly alive, totally aware of her own identity and conscious of her own worth. Such assurance arises from the experience of loving and being loved. Some women paradoxically become most sure of their identity when in fact they lose it in the life of another, taking on in marriage another's name and life-style, and finding the meaning of their own lives through sharing the lives of husband and children. Yet even within that identification there remains the need for a sense of personal identity, for 'room of one's own', as Virginia Woolf put it, in which one is aware of one's individual worth. I treasure especially the memory of one beautiful though deserted woman I met in a village in India whose dignity and sense of personal worth made an indelible impression upon me. She had neither husband nor child with whom to identify. In the eyes of many she would have seemed a pitiable person. She lived in a poverty-stricken community where her husband had left her because she was childless, she eked out a starvation-level existence on a wage of 10p a day, she was illiterate though very articulate. She told me in good evangelical language which I have never forgotten, 'Jesus Christ didn't only save me, he made me realize that my life was worth saving.'

What was Deena's life worth? To many she still seemed to be an 'outcaste', the old name for the community to which she belonged. To some she was now known by the prouder name of *harijan*, a child of God, as Mahatma Gandhi had insisted on calling the poorest of India's people. To a Christian doctor who had saved Deena's life by giving an emergency transfusion of her own blood when Deena had been desperately ill, she was a patient worth giving skill and blood to save. And to Deena herself, the full worth of her life was expressed in the words and acts of a Christian presbyter as he shared with her and with me broken pieces of bread and a common cup of wine, with the declaration of Jesus to us both: 'This is my body which is broken for you.

This is my blood which is shed for you.' We were both of the same value, bought with the same price, forgiven by the same love, given a unique worth. It was in that gospel that Deena, living as she was in all the deprivation of Asia, and I, sated with the affluence of the West, both found our essential identity. We were able to sing together the words of the Brahmin poet, Tilak, who found his salvation when he found Christ and expressed it thus:

> If there is aught of worth in me,
> It comes from Thee alone;
> Then keep me safe, for so, O Lord,
> Thou keepest but Thine own.[3]

It was in that experience of 'being kept safe' that we both found our identity and at the same time discovered our community with one another.

The section discussing questions of identity and culture at Bangkok came out with several affirmations of faith, hammered out of such personal experiences of Westerners and Easterners who believed that they had in a real sense come to themselves when they had come to Christ. They expressed it thus:

Christ came that I might be really me and that you might be really you,

Christ came to answer questions that I ask and not those which others think I ought to ask.

Christ came to question me as me.

Christ came because he wants me as I am, and you as you are to make us what we ought to be.

Christ came that you and I might grow into mature manhood measured by nothing less than the fullness of the stature of Christ himself.[4]

What a travesty it is if Christian preaching ever suggests that salvation means saving a person from himself, turning him into a totally different kind of being, modelled on the style and stance of the one from whom he receives the gospel. Jesus came not to destroy a person's identity, but to fulfil it. Conversion means turning from that self-centredness which is destructive to that self-discovery which is the creative embracing of a full and abundant life.

What is true of a person is true too of a people. Just as each person needs to discover his or her own identity, so each community needs to affirm its own cultural heritage. Too often the Christian gospel has been presented as a way of life shaped by the styles of Western culture. Even attempts at 'indigenizing' worship and proclamation have seemed to be like trying to dress up in local wrapping what was still essentially a foreign import. Truly indigenous worship and theology arises from the authentic experience of people who have discovered their own worth and the value of their own heritage as they see all things fulfilled in Christ.

This rediscovery of cultures brings reciprocal enrichment. In the West now poets, dramatists, artists are finding their imagination rekindled as the treasures of Eastern traditions are opened up before them. Western musicians tour Africa to listen spellbound to the drum-beats of ancient rhythms which bring new vitality to modern jazz. Holiday tourists find even their own hitherto unquestioned rules of etiquette affected by what they learn of the social customs and behaviour of people in other parts of the world.

Many of the assumptions made by Westerners about such sterling values as punctuality or the conventions of hospitality, for example, come under question in the light of other cultures. A Latin American at Bangkok reminded us of a cultural tradition which is fast being destroyed by the impact of Western concepts of time. To a Latin American *manyana*, literally 'tomorrow', traditionally meant some indefinite time in the future because, as he put it, 'for Latin Americans time is not lord over man but man is lord over time'. But now under the imposition of Anglo-Saxon ways of understanding time he said, 'We are running the risk of becoming fast and crazy at the same time.'

His words reminded me of the experience I had once in a jungle chapel in the Chin hills of Burma, where a Lushai congregation invited me to preach at their evening service. 'What time does it begin?' I asked, 'When the people come' was the obvious but to me startling reply! 'In Britain', I said, 'the steward would wait in the vestry with watch in his hand, priding himself on the punctuality of beginning the service precisely at 6.30.' 'What, even if the church wasn't full?' queried the Lushai. The logic of his question left me dumb.

Similarly, Western patterns of hospitality can be seen as disruptive of deeper values. A Nigerian girl, returning home after training as a nurse in Britain, was overheard telling her family of the strange ways of the English. 'They invite you as a guest for a certain day at a certain time. But if you can't make it and you turn up instead at any other time on another day you are not welcome.' It seemed a strange custom to a country where hospitality would be given whenever a stranger called.

Even so-called development can be destructive of culture. A European told me of a visit he made to a village in West Africa where he was challenged by a local community worker. 'You see that villager over there,' said the African to the European, 'he is sitting outside a house he has built himself, playing a stringed instrument he has made himself, singing a song he learned from his forefathers. If this were a so-called developed country, he would, I suppose, be sitting inside a pre-fab, watching on television a commercialized pop song. That is what I call cultural underdevelopment.'

The trouble is, as Gabriel Setiloane of South Africa put it at Bangkok, so much of Christian mission has been 'a one-way monologue' from the West. This, he maintained, has led to a seriously one-sided theology. For just as we are now discovering the real values of the diversity of our cultures, so too we need to realize the enrichment that comes to the whole theological spectrum as men and women reflect on the varieties of the experiences through which God has been making his ways known to mankind. He has not left himself without witness among the many nations of men. Today we see the emergence of theologies that arise out of the reflection of peoples upon their particular experience within the context of their own situations. From among the oppressed who have known all the indignity of dehumanization there has emerged a 'black theology', recognizing in Jesus one who also suffered oppression and who affirmed the worth and personhood of the lowliest and most despised, placing himself unequivocally on the side of the powerless. From women asserting their identity in a new way is emerging a 'feminine theology', reflecting on what it means to be female, made in the image of God, when so much theology has been fashioned from the standpoint of male experience and expressed in masculine images. Such theological pluralism should be seen not as a threat but as an enrichment to the whole ecumenical dialogue as we learn from one another the fullness of the gospel we proclaim. For it is only as we discover what the gospel means for each person in each place that it truly becomes a message of salvation for all people everywhere.

The way to such discovery lies along the path of a new humility. Kenneth Cragg, writing in the *International Review of Mission* in October 1969, warned Westerners of the dangers of a theology that is too small, too proud, too easy: 'There can be nothing larger than the heart of God, nothing surer than the particularity in Christ when that heart is read . . . We cannot have a wider reach than the narrow way nor a fuller compassion than the actual gospel.'

A century ago the missionaries' path was in a literal and physical sense a narrow way, a path hacked through the undergrowth into unknown territory, a path along which the missionary claimed to be bringing a totally new way of life. David Livingstone, for example, promised that along with Christianity he was bringing to Africa the blessing of commerce and of civilization, and to both those terms he inevitably gave the narrow definition of Western styles of commerce and a Western understanding of culture. Christianity was seen to have some special relation to the whole development of Western civilization so that the West seemed destined to dominate and determine all other cultures.

So along with the Christian faith was introduced into African societies a new individualism, a capitalistic economy, a Western culture and all these were seen to be integrally related. 'When the missionaries first came', a sceptical African is reported to have said, 'they had the Bibles and we had the land. Then they taught us to close our eyes and pray, and when we opened our eyes again, we had the Bibles and they had the land.'[7] However much Westerners may protest that this is a travesty of much that was done by men and women of sincere missionary motive and good intention, the fact remains that missionary expansion and Western colonialism were seen to come hand in hand into the newly opened continents of the nineteenth century. So it would not be surprising if, with the rejection of colonialism and the rediscovery of African and Asian identities, there had not been also a wholesale rejection of the Christian claims that seemed to be part of the whole Western package deal.

It is one of the miracles of grace that in the new Africa and Asia there are those who are finding that the Christian gospel, stripped of its Western accretions, is not alien to but expressive of the deepest realities of their own ancient cultures. A new ecumenical instinct is teaching us that all cultures have their value in helping us fully to understand our humanity in the light of the revelation of Christ. Gabriel Setiloane expresses his experience as both African and Christian in a haunting poem,[5] of which brief extracts can be quoted here. The God of Abraham and of Isaac is surely also the God of his African forefathers:

My father and theirs many generations before knew him.
They bowed the knee to him
By many names they knew him
And yet 'tis he the one and only God
They called him:
UVELING UAKI
  The First One
  Who came ere ever anything appeared:
UNKULUNKULU
  The Big Big One
  So big indeed that no space could ever contain him.
MODIMO
Because his abode is far up in the sky.
They also knew him as MODIRI
  For he has made all
and LESA
  The spirit without which the breath of man cannot be.

He goes on to recall the strange tales that reached his forefathers of a man of Bethlehem who went about doing good, but who was brought to Africa finally in Western disguise, which would have hidden him from African eyes had it not been for his suffering shared by so many African hearts and his sacrifice, recalling ancient African rites:

For ages he eluded us, this Jesus of Bethlehem, Son of Man
Going first to Asia and to Europe and the western sphere,
Some say he tried to come to us
    sending his messengers of old . . . But . . .
They were cut off by the desert and the great mountains of
    Ethiopia . . .
Later on he came, this Son of Man
Like a child delayed he came to us,
The white men brought him
He was pale, and not the sunburnt Son of the desert . . . and
    yet . . .
How like us he is this Jesus of Nazareth,
Beaten, tortured, imprisoned, spat upon, truncheoned
Denied by his own and chased like a thief in the night
Despised and rejected like a dog that has fleas
For no reason
No reason, but that he was Son of his Father.
Or . . . was there a reason?
There was indeed . . .
As in that sheep or goat we offer in sacrifice
Quiet and uncomplaining,
Its blood falling to the ground to cleanse it, as us,
And making peace between us and our fathers long passed away.
He is that lamb
His blood cleanses,
Not only us,
Not only the clan,
Not only the tribe,
But all, all mankind,
Black and white and brown and red
All mankind
He Jesus, Lord, Son of Man and Son of God,
Make peace with your blood and sweat and suffering
With God UVELINGUAKI, UNKULUNKULU
For the sins of mankind, our father and us,
That standing in the same sonship with all mankind and you,
Together with you we can pray to him above,
Father forgive.

So, as in our modern world we rediscover the ancient cultures we find how, in their deepest meaning, all human societies are relevant to one another. As Kenneth Cragg puts it: 'The religious cultures and histories of our common human world ought to have a living place in our properly Christian reckoning with our single contemporary history. To have it otherwise is to evacuate the humility of Christ and to jeopardize the sovereignty of the Spirit of God. There is no hemisphere that can become the globe.'

Can it be said then that there is a Christian identity transcending the personal, cultural and racial identity of each one of us? Two of the personal testimonies that emerged from the group at Bangkok were eloquent evidence of how such a Christian identity both includes and goes beyond the discovery of the worth of one's own being:

> In my country a white shop assistant smiles at her white customers, her face alive and alert. When she turns to me, her face and eyes go blank and she sees not a person but a black. Only by resisting, by fighting back, can I relate to her – and so I quarrel with her. I even hate her. But as a Christian I have to go beyond hate to the love that involves suffering, forgiveness and reconciliation.

> In my country, the solidarity of the state religion is tremendous. In becoming a Christian I made myself a second-class citizen. I lost my sense of belongingness. I am conscious that I am cut off from my own people like an uprooted tree. The answer of course is for the church to be there to belong to but in my case the church is not yet strong enough to give the sense of belongingness. The answer is to become more like Christ and accept suffering love and therefore to be liberated from all fetters and give back to the culture all the blessings that come through thirst.[6]

Belonging and not belonging – this experience of Christians throughout the ages has perhaps never been more vividly expressed than in the words of the anonymous letter-writer to Diognetus in the second century who, describing a group of Christians he had met, said of them: 'They share all things as citizens and suffer all things as aliens; they look upon their fatherland as though it were a foreign land, and upon every foreign land as though it were their fatherland.'

Thus we begin to come near to an understanding of what it means to be the new creation in Christ. It is not to be less than ourselves but more than ourselves, able to give and receive from those who are different from us, not in dependence upon one another. It is to recognize that all human experience, black and white, male and female, rich and poor finds its fulfilment and its transcendence in Jesus Christ – God dwelling with people, God present in and suffering with all our many humanities, God letting us be. In Jesus 'Being's source begins to be'. In commitment to him we find the courage to be and let be.

To let be, however, does not mean to leave alone. For our human fulfilment, we do not only need to discover our personal identity and to affirm our cultural heritage. We also need to come into mature relationship with others, particularly those of other identities, other cultures than ours. But it is so deeply a part of our nature to keep our distance from those who are different from ourselves that it takes a painfully radical process to undermine such stout walls of partition. Particularly is this so when we face those who do not even share our faith. How can we be both authentically Christian, naming the name of the One who we believe is the unique Saviour of all mankind and at the same time be truly human, affirming our common humanity with those whom we shut out by the very categories we apply to them? One of the German delegates at Bangkok reminded us of the origin of one of these categorical words:

The ancient Romans called the people living in villages outside the city the 'pagani', the backward people. My forefathers in the Germanic or Slavic forests of north and east Germany were called 'pagani' – uncivilized – by those living as Christians in the newly formed cities of mediaeval Europe. Later the word turned into 'pagan' and you know whom we called pagan. It was not in the first place the non-Christian in a theological sense. It was the people without – without our knowledge, without our ethics, without our strength, without our standards, without presumably the grace given to us. Calling them pagans we actually paganized them. In our humble attempts at dialogue we are about to reverse this unjustified process. If dialogue was nothing else than just depaganization it would be worth trying if only for our own sake, or let me say for our own salvation.

Dialogue with others is an essential part of the discovery of the identity both of ourselves and of the others. An Old English expression describes conversation as 'discovering oneself to another'. If we are truly to discover our own faith, the reason for the hope that is in us, we shall do so only in relation to people of other faiths, as we approach them with humility and with readiness to learn from them the reason for their hopes and fears, their search for salvation. If we truly believe that Christ is the Way, the Truth and the Life, that no man comes to the Father except by him, then we must follow his tracks wherever he is leading men to a knowledge and love of God, whether they name him as their Lord or not. He draws us along with him, into relationship with others, both for their sake and for our own. Stanley Samartha, who is in charge of the World Council of Churches sub-unit on Dialogue with men of living faiths and ideologies, has said:

There are at least three theological reasons why dialogue is and ought to be a continuing Christian concern. First, God in Christ Jesus has himself entered into relationship with men of all faiths and all ages offering the good news of salvation. The incarnation is God's dialogue with men. To be in dialogue is therefore to be part of God's continuing work among us and our fellowmen. Second, the offer of a true community inherent in the gospel through forgiveness, reconciliation and a new creation, and of which the church is a sign and a symbol, inevitably leads to dialogue. The freedom and love which Christ offers constrain us to be in fellowship with strangers so that all may become fellow citizens in the household of God. Third, there is the promise of Jesus Christ that the Holy Spirit will lead us into all truth. Since truth in the biblical understanding is not propositional but relational and is to be sought not in the isolation of lonely meditation but in the living personal confrontation between God and man, and men and men, dialogue becomes one of the means of the quest for truth. And, because Christians cannot claim to have a monopoly of truth, we need to meet men of other faiths and ideologies as part of our trust in the obedience to the promises of Christ.[7]

For most people today in our pluralistic societies the meeting with people of other faiths and ideologies is now not a matter of choice but of necessity. The choice is whether to enter into any meaningful relationship with them or not. Only as we do so shall we fully share our common humanity. So dialogue cannot be left to the theologians or the philosophers. It is a contact of life with life without which all life is impoverished.

An interesting experience of dialogue at a lay, non-professional level has taken place over the last three years at a summer school here in Britain. It happened by accident that the lay training school of the Methodist Church and the summer school of the Communist Party had booked for the same week at the Conference Centre in Swanwick a few years ago. At first the encounter was greeted with scarcely veiled hostility from both sides. Christians arriving at the wrong registration desk showed emotions ranging from fear to outrage when they were innocently asked if they were party members. Marxists sat down in noisy protest when Christians remained standing to sing grace. And in the first couple of days there was an inhuman kind of apartheid with an invisible iron curtain drawn across the dining room and carefully averted gazes in the corridors lest any Christians make eye contact with a Marxist! But then someone suggested a joint discussion, 'purely academic of course', between the two groups on the subject of the Marxist–Christian dialogue. So a solemn joint meeting was duly held, long and carefully documented addresses were given and then at last real conversation began. In the process of debate admittedly we learned little more about either Marxism or Christianity but a lot more about each other. The fascinating thing was to discover how much alike we were. We both had our fundamentalists, our fanatics, our radicals, our moderates. It was often possible to tell, from the stance and the style of a person rising to address the meeting, which of those groups he belonged to even before it became clear whether he was a Marxist or a Christian! We discovered too that we both had our stereotypes about the other which blinded us to our common humanity. Methodists expected every Marxist to carry a hand grenade while Marxists expressed relief that Methodists do on occasions lay aside their hymn books! But the miracle that happened was that across the division friendships were made which have lasted through the years, and reached depths of intimacy and sharing of faith which would never have been possible outside the relationship initiated in dialogue. Now three years later the tradition of a dialogue session is a permanent feature of the programme of both summer schools as a means of humanizing our presence together in the same place at the same time and a sharing of our deepest concerns, conflicts, commitments with one another.

In our most recent meeting together we took as one of the bases of our discussion an essay that has arisen out of the Marxist–Christian dialogue in France, in which the Marxist philosopher Roger Garaudy writes of how the story of Jesus sounds to him. As we discussed this together, the Christians among us learned again how in dialogue with others we discover anew the essentials of our faith freed from the cultural and historical trappings that have for so long encumbered them. It was as if we too were listening to a new story:

> In the time of the Emperor Tiberius's reign – no one knows exactly when or where – an individual whose name is not known suddenly opened up new horizons to men.
>
> Quite certainly he was neither a philosopher nor a tribune, but he had to live in such a way that his entire life would signify that each one of us can, at any moment, make a new start.
>
> Dozens, perhaps even hundreds of popular story-tellers have spread abroad the good news. We know three or four of them.
>
> The shock they received was expressed in the images of simple people, of the insulted and the injured, of the sad at heart, when they dream that all things have become possible: the blind who begin to see, the paralyzed who walk for the first time, the hungry in the wilderness who are given bread, the prostitute in whom the woman is awakened, the dead child brought back to life.
>
> So that the good news could be proclaimed to the full, it was necessary for this man to tell the world, through his resurrection, that every frontier, even the ultimate frontier of death itself, had been overcome.
>
> Some scholar or other may question every fact of this man's

life, but that will alter nothing of this certainty which changes life. A fire has been lit. It bears living witness to the spark or the original flame which gave it birth.

First of all the fire was a rising of the wretched: if this had not been so, the 'establishment' from Nero to Diocletian, would not have dealt so hardly with them.

With this man, love had to be militant and subversive: if this had not been so, he, the first, would not have been crucified.

Until then, all the wise men had meditated on destiny, on necessity confused with reason. He showed them their folly. He who was the reverse of destiny, who was liberty, creation, life – he took the inevitability out of history.

He fulfilled the promises of the heroes and martyrs of the great awakening to freedom. Not only the hopes of Isaiah or the wrath of Ezekiel. Prometheus was unbound. Antigone freed from her prison walls. These chains and walls, mythical images of destiny, crumbled to dust before him. All the gods were dead and man began.

It was as if man had been born again.

I look upon this cross, symbol of this new birth and I dream of all who have widened the horizons: of St John of the Cross, who taught us to discover everything by virtue of having nothing, of Karl Marx who showed us how we could change the world, of Van Gogh and of all who made us realize that man is too great to be sufficient unto himself.

You, the beneficiaries of the great hope of which Constantine robbed us, men of the church, give him back to us! His life and death belong to us, too, to all for whom that hope has meaning, to all who learned from him that man is created as creator.[8]

Equally important as the Marxist–Christian dialogue is the growing dialogue with other faiths. At Bangkok many people took the opportunity of an experience of dialogue with Buddhists, visiting a nearby Buddhist monastery, listening to a senior Buddhist monk explaining the Buddhist way of meditation, meeting with Buddhist laymen who explained their faith and life. They tried in the process to be as eager to listen as to speak, ready both to rejoice in the discovery of common ground and equally to explore the differences, trying to remember the Lord's promise that the Holy Spirit will lead into all truth. Inevitably in the discussions afterwards some felt an inescapable tension between dialogue and evangelism. Others affirmed that there need be no such tension. A desire to share and a readiness to let others share with us should inspire our witness to Christ. For today mission is not the prerogative of Christians alone. In the report of the section on dialogue it was said:

There are missionary activities of many religions in lands outside their countries of origin and tradition. At the same time there is a universal search for a new identity. Because of this reciprocal mission, world mission may once more become acceptable as an authentic expression of Christian faith and not be open to the charge of religious imperialism. The resulting confrontation and dialogue will lead to deeper understanding, the clearing away of ignorance about each other and a sharpening of the imperative of commitment.[9]

Dialogue is seen here as another open, loving way of letting people be themselves as we honestly share with one another our common search for salvation. Let the last word in this chapter come from a personal testimony given at Bangkok by Murray Rogers, an English missionary who has lived a lifetime of identification with Indian people and who, speaking of his Hindu friends, told us: 'Knowing me and knowing that I love Christ a little they ask me things about my experience, and suddenly sometimes something happens in them and they see that the one whom they love, the one in whose presence they have spent hours of contemplation, is precisely the one towards whom I am pointing in my experience. The veil comes off not because of what I say but because the spirit at that second makes the bells ring in the other man's mind.'

So does the spirit let us be, releasing us into the full maturity of our selfhood and at the same time enabling us to discover ourselves in dialogue with one another, leading us on to that fullness of our identity which is realized in the new community in Christ.

7

Bread, Freedom and Faith

Salvation and Social Justice

'Soup, soap and salvation belong together', declared William Booth, founder of the Salvation Army. In that deceptively simple remark Booth was giving to this one word 'salvation' a much fuller significance than even some of those who beat his drums have recognized. The offer of salvation has involved the Salvation Army in the development not only of a militant programme of proclamation but also in an elaborate and highly efficient network of relief operations, social services and disciplined communities of faith and witness stretching out across the whole world.

'Bread, freedom and faith' might be a modern equivalent of Booth's definition of the content of salvation. Good news for the poor, liberty for the oppressed, sight for the blind – these were key themes of Jesus' own manifesto as he announced the good news in Nazareth (Luke 4). Nothing could be more relevant in our contemporary world, where increasing economic exploitation produces more poor people than ever before, where political domination enslaves greater masses of oppressed people and where the combination of religious apathy and secular affluence leave many people blind to any vision of a changed order of society.

Christians have been entrusted, as M. M. Thomas has put it, with 'the utopian vision' of what human community could be. Theirs is the responsibility for helping to carry out practical programmes by which that vision can be translated into reality for all mankind. The problems that such programmes involve, such as matters of political strategy, of community development, of violent struggle and non-violent resistance, of the establishment of law and order, of national planning, all feature in the biblical story of salvation, as again and again prophets recalled the people of God to the utopian vision of a society where 'justice and peace have kissed one another', and people 'do justly, love mercy and walk humbly with their God'. A concern for salvation today inevitably means a concern for the struggle for social justice in our time, in its local, national and international manifestations. In some situations Christians are deeply identified with the struggles of the oppressed. In others they are associated with the maintenance of the *status quo*. In no situation can they be neutral so long as they proclaim that this world is the arena of God's action and that now is the day of salvation.

Significantly, it was the section dealing with Salvation and Social Justice at Bangkok that came out with the strongest theological statement of any of the sections. Beginning with Jesus' sermon at Nazareth it went on to point out that through Christ men and women are liberated from the prison of guilt and of apathy, and are empowered with all their energies and possibilities to share in his messianic work. Through his death on the cross the hope of salvation becomes realistic, facing unflinchingly the reality of sin which is at the heart of all injustice; through his resurrection from the dead, the reality of salvation becomes hopeful, for he has inaugurated already the new age in which the Kingdom of God and of free people is at hand. Faith in Christ releases in us creative freedom for the salvation of the world. Christ has taken the inevitability out of history. He so liberates us from sin and fear and despair that we are free to create our own future and to share in shaping the destiny of all mankind.

It was this section above all that stressed the wholeness of the meaning of salvation:

> The salvation which Christ brought, and in which we partici-
> pate, offers a comprehensive wholeness in this divided life. We
> understand salvation as newness of life – the unfolding of true
> humanity in the fullness of God (Col. 2.9). It is salvation of the
> soul and the body, of the individual and society, mankind and
> 'the groaning creation' (Rom. 8.19). As evil works both in per-
> sonal life and in exploitative social structures which humiliate
> humankind, so God's justice manifests itself both in the justi-
> fication of the sinner and in social and political justice. As guilt
> is both individual and corporate so God's liberating power
> changes both persons and structures. We have to overcome the
> dichotomies in our thinking between soul and body, person and
> society, human kind and creation. Therefore we see the struggles
> for economic justice, political freedom and cultural renewal as
> elements in the total liberation of the world through the mission
> of God. This liberation is finally fulfilled when 'death is swal-
> lowed up in victory' (I Cor. 15.55). This comprehensive notion
> of salvation demands of the whole of the people of God a match-
> ing comprehensive approach to their participation in salvation.'[1]

To be saved, then, means to be free to share in the saving work of Christ. What does that mean today for churches, as companies of people who claim his salvation? Are they themselves truly free? Or have they so much vested interest in the present order of things that they cannot effectively be agents of salvation in society? In some parts of the world, the churches themselves seem inevitably bound up with the interests of the dominant class, the ruling power, the privi-leged groups within society – a part of the establishment actively supporting economically and even morally policies that perpetuate the privilege of the few at the expense of the many. In other places, by inactivity and silence in face of injustice and oppression, the church is equally guilty of complicity with evil. In a few places, churches have identi-fied with the struggle of the oppressed. All Christians and all churches need to examine themselves as to whether they do serve Christ and his saving work alone, or whether they are trying to serve two masters and have become so enslaved by mammon and so concerned about their own self-preservation, that they are no longer free to resist effectively that exploitation that enslaves so many of their fellow men. The true community of Christ would be one that counts all things loss for the sake of the Kingdom. The truly charismatic church would be one so filled with the spirit that its energies would be activated towards the salvation of all mankind (I Cor. 12). The fully liberated church would be one which initiated actions for the liberation of all peoples without calculating self-interest. 'We seek a church which is the catalyst of God's saving work in the world', said the Bangkok report, 'a church which is not merely the refuge of the saved but a community serving the world in the love of Christ.'[2]

Within the struggle for social justice the three dimensions represented by bread, freedom and faith are all integrally related to one another. There is a sense in which it is true, as D. T. Niles has said, that 'the only way in which God dare appear to a hungry man is in the form of bread', and salvation must be concerned with the struggle against the economic exploitation which keeps two-thirds of the world hungry and the other third overfed. Yet it is equally true that man does not live by bread alone, and it is from among the poorest people on earth that we hear the claim that it is not merely better wages that would save them, but rather a recognition of their full human dignity and political rights. Salvation, then, is concerned with the liberation of people from that political oppression that enslaves them and makes them less than men. Yet it is equally true again that political freedom of itself does not ensure a fully humane and happy society. It is often in the so-called 'free' nations of the world that there is a growing sense of despair, of apathy, of helplessness. So salvation is concerned with the rediscovery of faith, the rebirth of hope, the eradicating of sin, sin that is manifested in the greed, the tyranny, the fear that are the roots of poverty, oppression and despair in the world.

This work of salvation, which is one work, begins at different points in the different situations within history. Nobody can do in every particular situation everything at the same time. There is need to discern the point of entry at which the

Spirit of God beckons us to join him in his saving work. At Bangkok we heard testimony from people actively involved in different kinds of struggle for social justice and tried to discern what these situations say to us as Christians about our priorities in proclaiming salvation today.

We began with the most difficult, places where change is being brought about in unjust situations by violent and revolutionary means. Immediately this raises for Christians the age-old dilemma as to whether violence is ever justified as a means of bringing liberation. For those who were with us in Bangkok this was no mere academic debate. We had an African Christian laying his life on the line in a liberation movement in Angola, where the battle against Portuguese oppression is bloody and brutal; we had a Protestant and a Catholic from Northern Ireland caught daily in the cross-fire of rival and sometimes indiscriminate violence; we had a North Vietnamese Christian working at the time in the torn and tense city of Saigon. What did it mean to speak of salvation in any of these situations?

The one thing that became clear in the discussion of all these issues was that violence breeds violence in a vicious circle of devastation. In each situation there was discernible not only the rebel violence provoked by injustice but also the legalized violence perpetuating oppression. Violence which grew out of frustration exploded into reckless disregard of life, countered by increasing brutality, all of which comes under the condemnation of the gospel (Mark 5.43–48). But whether violence is ever justified either to preserve a relatively just order or to attack an unjust one remains a deep dilemma for the Christian conscience.

Among us at Bangkok were expressed three quite different views. There were those who took a persistently pacifist position, declaring that violence in any form can never be consistent with obedience to Jesus Christ. They made a clear distinction between pacifism and passivism, however. The non-violent action which they advocated as a means of resisting oppression or bringing about social change would be positive, courageous and sacrificial, and should be judged not by the measure of its success as a strategy but by its faithfulness as a witness to the invincible love and transcendent power of Jesus, which is its only justification.

There were others who were prepared to grant that in extreme circumstances Christians might be justified in taking part in violence. They recognized the possibility of the 'just war' and were prepared to acknowledge that there could also be the possibility of the 'just revolution'. Their emphasis, however, was on the word 'just' – Christians must be fully convinced of the justice of the cause for which they were fighting and must also firmly believe that there was no other possibility open to them for furthering that cause. Moreover, they must be assured that the violence would lead effectively to the establishment of a more just order and that it did not itself become the means of perpetuating injustice.

For the third group, the choice of violence or non-violence was no longer an option. Trapped in situations where violence was already rampant, they could not escape from being involved in it either actively or passively. They saw their Christian responsibility as being to work to reduce the sum total of violence as much as possible and to do all they could to enable people to enter again into just and peaceful relations with each other.

Since the Bangkok Conference, a report on this whole subject of *Violence, Non-Violence and the Struggle for Social Justice* has been brought to the Central Committee of the World Council of Churches. Recognizing the three attitudes described above, the report makes no attempt to judge between them. Rather it reminds all Christians, whatever positions they take in seeking either to change the structures of society or to defend them, of the value of mutual challenge and discussion and the recognition that different situations may call for different responses. To aid this process of challenge and self-examination, the report suggested certain key questions each group of Christians should ask themselves about their own action in situations of injustice, along the following lines:

Those who would be prepared to use violence against an unjust order should ask:

– Have we really first explored all the possibilities for non-violent action?

– How can we prevent the methods we are using from themselves becoming instruments of dehumanization?

– How shall we integrate our former oppressors and their families into the new society we are fighting for?

Those who advocate non-violence as a matter of principle should ask:

– Do we realize how deeply entrenched is the violence in the structures of society, and how socially disruptive any resistance to it will need to be?

– Is there any danger of our giving the means (non-violence) priority over the end sought (justice)?

– Are we more concerned with our own good conscience or with the good of the oppressed?

Those who, by whatever means, are working for the destruction of an existing power structure in order to build a better one should ask:

– What result do we expect, and is this worth the price to be paid?

– How do we keep checks on our own power so that we do not in turn become oppressive?

– How will our opponents be integrated into the new society?

Those who basically are concerned with preserving and defending the institutions of an existing society should ask:

– Are we acting in the light of the biblical concern for the poor and oppressed, or for the preservation of our own group-interest?

– How far does the violence entrenched in society differ from that of revolutionary groups?

Those Christians who live in countries where there is opportunity to influence and change the structures of government, industry and society in the interests of social justice should ask:

– Are there groups in our society who are voiceless and excluded from exerting influence?

– How far is a fundamental dislocation of the powers-that-be needed if full justice is to be achieved?

74

The most important question, however, is not directed to any of these groups alone, but by all of them together to the whole church. The problem is not primarily that some Christians act violently for justice and peace, while others act non-violently. The greater problem is that most Christians are not acting on the matter at all. The real questions therefore to pose to all Christians are:

– How are we translating our commitment to Jesus Christ as Lord into specific social and political engagement for social justice?

– How do we find our places as servants of the servant Lord alongside all people who are concerned with human freedom and fulfilment?

As we tried to apply these criteria to the situations described at Bangkok, it soon became clear how different each situation was and how essential it is to work out within the situation what would be a realistic work for salvation. The Christian from Angola interpreted salvation in terms of the independence of the African peoples and the right to decide their own destiny – an independence which at present there seemed no other possible way of achieving except by military action; though alongside this the liberation movement stresses also the importance of programmes of education and welfare among the oppressed people. Christians from Northern Ireland spoke of salvation in terms of justice and reconciliation, a prospect which was made more remote by continuing violence and which cried out for political solutions. The Christian from Vietnam saw salvation in terms of peace which alone would provide the opportunity of reconstructing a shattered society.

In each situation too the churches were seen to have played different roles. We were reminded of how Portuguese Catholic missions had been described in the Vatican–Portuguese Missionary Accord of 1940 as 'considered to be of imperial usefulness; they have an eminently civilizing influence. Missionary congregations, apart from the help they receive from the Holy See, will be financed according to need by the government of Portugal and the respective Colony.' Such ecclesiastical undergirding of an oppressive

75

political power had led to the church's becoming, in the words of the General Council of the White Fathers, 'a counter-witness in a country which openly proclaims itself Catholic and Protector of the church but in the long run is using the church for aims which have nothing to do with the Gospel of Jesus Christ'. It was the basic ambiguity of that situation that led the White Fathers in Africa to decide in May 1971 to withdraw all their missionaries from the Portuguese territory of Mozambique.

We heard too a report from the American Task Force on Angola comprised of Mission Board executives in the USA and Canada, together with some Angolans living in America, who had been examining the connection between the past and future action of the Boards in relation to the Angola Liberation Movement and their primary responsibility for world mission. The task force states clearly its conviction that 'God wills liberation for Angola and for the world and affirms the need for mission boards and churches to express solidarity with the liberation struggle'. Its recommendations fall into two main areas: first, to reduce the support which the USA and Canada and other allies give to Portuguese colonialism, by promoting a programme of education, political and economic action within their own countries; second, to increase the support for Angola liberation movements by making a strong financial and material commitment to them as distinct from merely aiding refugees. Their report concludes: 'As Christians we believe that God, as revealed in Jesus Christ, is active in the liberation struggle in Angola. Angolans themselves will be the main instrument of this liberation. Although our role is secondary, it is still serious and significant.'[3]

Delegates from Northern Ireland, both Catholic and Protestant, while emphasizing that theirs was not primarily a religious conflict despite the religious labels attached to the two sides, yet saw the churches as sharing responsibility for much of what had happened by having given silent consent through the years to an illogical and unjust political philosophy. The comments of two retired Protestant ministers of religion were quoted: 'As I look back upon my ministry my greatest regret is that I failed to speak out against injustices which I knew were being practised' . . . 'I blame the Catholic leaders. If only they had told us they felt discriminated against we could have done something about it' . . .

For almost fifty years the Catholics of Northern Ireland had taken no part in Northern Ireland politics. Stormont (the Ulster seat of government) was described by Lord Carson, its chief architect, as a 'Protestant parliament for a Protestant people', and Catholics were encouraged by their church to accept this as the will of God, wherein prevailing injustices should be accepted without question as a Christian obligation. It was the newly formed civil rights movement which in 1967 began to rock the conscience of the government, the church and many Christians as they demanded equal rights for all.

> The younger ones insisted it was not enough to pray and carry out remedial charitable endeavours to bind the wounds of the suffering, but that charity and justice must be rebuilt into laws and institutions by specific political and economic structures. If this could not be done by legal and constitutional means then civil disobedience, passive or active resistance, must be used. Perhaps at this critical point if the church had been seen to be leading the people in their demands for social justice it would have had more influence, but from then on it seemed many clergy were almost in the position caricatured in the question, 'Where is that crowd going? For I am its leader'![4]

Since then the situation has escalated into violence on both sides, and both the Catholic and Protestant delegates at Bangkok paid eloquent tribute to the courage and dedication of priests, ministers and laity of both churches in the work of reconciliation and relief they have done throughout the troubles. It is as though through disaster the real life of the church is being reborn and it is re-discovering the meaning of being a 'servant church'. But brave words and good deeds are being drowned by the noise of bombing and shooting and the question is whether the churches' involvement now has come too little and too late.

The third violent situation was the one closest at hand to us in Bangkok, the war in Vietnam. In this situation, there had been no shortage of statements by church leaders, and the Conference, after the agonizing debate already described in this book, was to add one more, saying:

> This seemingly unending war puts a heavy burden on our Conference. How do we acclaim the saving and liberating work of God when many of us are, in one way or another, part of its denial? How can we preach the good news of Salvation Today, when on the same day a holocaust of destruction is unleashed which is widely believed by its perpetrators to be a defence of freedom and Christian values? How can we discuss the missionary strategy of the Christian church in our time when millions of Asians are faced with the brutal power politics of countries, some of which are made up predominantly of people who profess Christianity?[5]

Tribute was paid to the leadership of American churches in protesting against the war and in the support they had given to those who refused to pay taxes or to serve in the armed forces and who had demonstrated in other ways a commitment to end the war. Now it urged that the Fund for Reconstruction and Reconciliation in Indo-China recently brought into being by the World Council of Churches should become an unmistakable sign of repentance and willingness by Christians all over the world to give sacrificially to assist the Vietnamese people's own efforts in rebuilding what has been destroyed.

The story of the salvation of the people of God was not confined to the violent episodes in the Exodus story. Equally daunting were the long years in the wilderness, the search for manna and sustenance, and the sheer daily problem of providing bread for people living in poverty. Today there are more undernourished, illiterate, diseased people in the world than at any time in history, and this following a so-called 'Development Decade' in which the nations were supposed to be committed to international co-operation to counteract the economic exploitation whereby the rich get richer and the poor get poorer both within nations and across the whole world community.

So in the section on Salvation and Social Justice at Bangkok we also focussed our attention on the efforts of those attempting to counteract this kind of exploitation. We looked especially at the work of groups active within affluent nations to raise the awareness of peoples there as to how poverty is perpetuated through international systems of trade and investment. How do churches, who for so long have seen their mission in terms of feeding the hungry, healing the sick, educating the illiterate, relate to such endeavours which are directed not merely at the alleviation of human suffering but at the removal of its cause? The debate about investments in firms operating directly in Southern Africa, which had been so fully pursued at the World Council of Churches' Central Committee in Utrecht in 1972, was continued here and the Bangkok Conference fully endorsed and commended to missionary societies, the recommendation of the Central Committee that church bodies holding investments in firms operating within Southern Africa should use their influence actively to try to persuade those firms to withdraw their interests and thus weaken an economy which depends so much for its strength upon external support and internal exploitation.

One very active group in the Netherlands was represented at Bangkok by the Rev. H. van Andel, Secretary of the 'X minus Y' movement. He described this as a movement of anticipation, that is, a movement that invited people to do voluntarily what ought to be done by their Government and is not yet done. It began in an unusual and unexpected way – a protest against a cut in income tax! The Government of the Netherlands, as a result of favourable economic growth, was able to decrease government taxation in the fifties. Yet at the same time there was no increase in government aid for developing countries. So some people in protest sent back to the Ministry of Finance the money they had gained by the cut in income tax and insisted that it be used for development aid. Later, the campaign concentrated on the UN aim that rich countries should give 1% of their national income as development aid. In 1968 a self-tax was introduced, whereby people voluntarily paid a sum representing the difference between the percentage of Dutch National Income to which poor countries have a minimal right ('X') minus the percentage of Dutch National Income which is actually spent on official development aid ('Y'). The sum represented by X minus Y has been spent in ways which are intended to point the way forward to government and non-governmental agencies towards positive ways of expressing aid – for example, through the United Nations Capital Development Fund whereby gifts and long-term loans are made available to help increase capital in developing countries, with no strings attached; through aid to liberation movements in Southern Africa; through world shops within the Netherlands itself where products from developing countries are sold together with the story about the unjust trade arrangements relating to those products and thus exposing exploitation; and through a special fund which makes possible initiatives of small scope which are in general not acceptable to donor agencies because of their political nature or emergency character. It was hoped that other development action groups, churches, trade unions and others might adopt similar programmes to X minus Y, not simply as a means of making money available but as in itself a means of education about economic exploitation and of bringing pressure to bear upon governments to achieve their stated aim for development aid.

A third area of activity that came under discussion in the concern for salvation and social justice was participation in national planning that is designed to produce better conditions of human life and community. Churches with long-established programmes of welfare, medical and educational work are now involved with national plans for the development of such services and the changing of social structures. In many cases the planners have overtaken the pioneers. But questions need to be raised as to how social needs are assessed and how far communities themselves participate in the plans for urban development, for health care services, for education. So far as urban development is concerned, the iniquity of land profiteering and speculation makes urgent the necessity for urban land to be in the main publicly owned. Everywhere in the world a major problem in cities is the provision of housing, a problem which is not met by planning alone. People need more than blocks of tenements if they are to live fully human lives. Sensitivity to the social and cultural values of the people being rehoused and to the needs of special groups within society such as the elderly or the handicapped would be a saving grace in providing a happier and more humane urban environment.

Sensitivity also to the real needs in health service of rural communities could literally save many more lives if the planners would only set aside some of their more grandiose schemes and concentrate instead on community care and community development. Too often the temptation has been to copy the Western tendency to build bigger and better centralized hospitals and to spend more and more specialized skill on fewer and fewer patients. But in areas where over half the children still die before they are five years old from diseases which are nearly all preventable such as malnutrition, diarrhoea, pneumonia, only a very small proportion of the population can benefit from a hospital service, and a vast amount of human suffering goes un-relieved unless the whole community joins in a concern for total health-needs. Dr Forbes of Jamaica, who is Senior Lecturer on Child Health in the University of East Africa, described to the section at Bangkok a community effort being made to meet health-needs in a small coastal village about sixty miles south of Dar-es-Salaam in Tanzania. Here a clinic was established which all children in the village were encouraged to attend at regular intervals. A mobile team of doctors, nurses, record-keeper, health and nutrition educator, and driver visited the clinic weekly, where over 2000 children were registered. But the key to the clinic's working was in the co-operation of the community itself who shared the responsibility for running it. The village chief sat by the doctor helping to undress babies and listening to the medical histories. Another man, a former leprosy patient, looked after the distribution of dried milk supplies, another organized the weighing and so on. After each clinic the Citizens' Health Committee met to discuss such matters as timing, school health, attitudes of the mobile team, infant feeding and so on. The health of the children improved noticeably and a new pride developed in the whole life of the village. Mothers lost their anxieties, children grew strong and healthy, and the whole community enjoyed a sense of achievement and well-being. Life was being saved and they were sharing in the saving of it.

An area of national life in which missions have so far played a large part is education. In what way can schools be said to be part of God's plan of salvation? Sometimes they have seemed to be places where the younger generation is merely trained to adapt itself to and accept the values of an older one, or, in the case of mission schools, an alien culture. Yet the real aim of education should be to make people aware of their own potential, to value their own culture, and to encourage them to see the choices they must make if they are to shape the kind of society which will best serve the needs of their community. 'The aim of education', said the Bangkok report, 'should be the empowering of the powerless, giving voice to the voiceless, developing full human beings and integrating persons, going on throughout the whole of life.' It was urged that educational experiment and research should go on in all six continents, with great attention being given to the use of mother tongue as well as modern languages and cultures. Educational planning needs to involve wider ranges of people than just professional teachers and politicians, so that the concerns of the whole community may be served, and the education available can be related to the needs of all the people, not just a favoured few. Christian teachers should always be on the look out for ways and methods whereby the work they share in shall really be saving people's humanity, not simply preserving society's values.

Community development was thus seen as another vital part of the work for salvation and social justice. Enabling people to define their own needs, to decide on their own goals and to develop their own resources and strategies for achieving them is an essential part of empowering them with that 'life more abundant' which is their divine right. Those with a true sense of Christian mission must learn genuinely to work *with* people rather than *for* people, enabling those who thought they had no power to discover the power that is within them. An integral part of good news for the poor is the encouragement of those who have for so long passively accepted a destiny of misery to realize that the door to the future is open to them if they will only ask, seek, knock against the present structures of injustice.

This has been the aim of a project such as Centro Sviluppo 2 in Sicily, where farming communes have been established to help stem the tide of emigration into the industrial northern parts of Italy and to develop new forms of working collectively on the farms. These new farms not only make possible better agricultural methods, they also enable farm workers to take a new pride in their profession and to discover their own potential as a force for economic and political change in a society where they have so often been the victims of exploitation. Another project described at Bangkok was the Zone One Tondo Organization in Manila among the urban poor, representing about 100 people's organizations with over 80,000 members discovering how best to bring about change in the slum conditions in which so many of them are compelled to live.

In each of these projects and many others like them the primary concern is to raise the level of awareness of those at the bottom of society's pyramid. They need to be helped to understand the nature of the forces that press down upon them and to realize what they can and must do to improve the quality and condition of their lives. Thus an important role of the church in society is seen to be the relating of community action groups to one another in ways of discovering together what it means today to have a mission to the poor. A church which would be truly obedient to its Lord must take seriously to heart his requirements – 'to loose the fetters of injustice, to untie the knots of the yoke, to snap every yoke and set free those who have been crushed' (Isa. 58.6 NEB). No doubt such activity must result in an upheaval of the whole structure of society, when the small people are magnified and the mighty are put down from their seats, when the hungry are filled with good things and the rich are sent empty away. But was not this the promise that heralded the coming of our salvation?

8

All Together Now

Salvation and Mission in a Divided World

One way of rediscovering the meaning of an old word is to examine the new contexts in which it is used. In a word-association game recently a congregation was asked to give their immediate response to three words which have come back into currency today. The first was 'space', and the response immediately was 'man', 'ship' or 'station'. The second following straight on was 'mission' and the response came back, 'control' or 'project'. The third was 'salvation' with the unanimous response 'army'.

That congregation thus demonstrated clearly that they belonged to the twentieth century! Their great-grandfathers would have given quite different responses, more 'religious' ones probably. Space no doubt would have been linked not so much with man as with God, or at least with dimensions of time and eternity; mission would almost certainly have been associated with the sending of missionaries by church or mission board; while salvation would have been thought of primarily as a theological concept rather than a military-type operation.

Today space-travel has so widened human horizons that even the moon is thought of as man's domain. One of the most effective missionary addresses I ever heard was given recently at the United Methodist Conference in Atlanta,

Georgia, by a reticent young layman who seemed extremely nervous at facing a vast congregation. He need not have been, for he had the most arresting opening sentence I have ever heard. 'Last year,' he began, 'I spent thirty-six hours walking on the moon.' From that moment Alan Bean had the whole congregation spell-bound as he described how the exploration of space had for him enlarged his understanding of the nature of God and the cosmic design. But what was most memorable was his account of the return to earth, that planet which from a distance looked so incredibly beautiful and so pathetically small. The space-craft in which he was travelling was badly damaged. There was serious danger that it would never make the return journey. Then came through the messages from mission control at Houston. 'The whole world is holding its breath,' the spacemen were told, 'willing you back safely.' Somehow the concentrated thoughts and energies of the millions of people watching with such concern the fragile journey seemed almost like a magnetic force holding the space-craft on its course, drawing it down to a successful landing. It was a parable, said Alan Bean, of what prayer could mean in the world today as the energies of millions across the world are concentrated together on the prayer 'Thy Kingdom come, Thy will be done on earth.'

Such are the cosmic dimensions of man's exploration to-day. In the midst of it stands mission control, a vast network of communications, an intricate team of different kinds of technical, medical, human skills working together on one major project, a transmitting station receiving and sending signals from base to explorer and from explorer back to base. Is there not a new image here of what the word 'mission' might most fully convey as the role of the church in our contemporary world? Emilio Castro, summing up the Conference on Salvation Today, said:

> We are at the end of a missionary era; we are at the very beginning of the world mission. We have heard here harsh words on the missionary enterprise. But now it is more than emotion – it is theological reflection. The affirmation of African culture, the conveying of Indian spirituality, the challenge to

social revolution are the starting points for a new day in world mission. The cry for help from brothers and sisters in Europe, the expression of concern for world mission by delegates of socialist countries all invite us to a new day. Our mood should not be frustration but one of joyous anticipation.

How is this mission to the ends of the earth related to the life of the church at the end of the street? In what way does that local company see itself as part of a world-wide army of salvation? The first need is for each local church to realize that it is itself both mission field and mission centre. No longer does it make any sense to distinguish between 'sending' and 'receiving' churches so far as mission is concerned. Every church needs both to send and to receive. Within its local community each congregation needs to be a kind of nerve-centre, picking up the signals of need, monitoring where the action is happening, quick to move at the impulses of love manifesting itself within the neighbourhood. As it transmits the gospel, it will do so clearly in the words of preaching and the symbols of sacraments, through the power of prayer and the service of intercession, in the lives of people acting out the truths of the gospel in their relations with one another and in their wider communities:

> A local congregation that lives to itself sabotages the saving action of God in the neighbourhood; one that exposes itself to share the needs and aspirations of its neighbourhood and to join with others in relevant action is an instrument of God's salvation, enabling men and women to find in Jesus Christ ultimate meaning and sacredness for their lives. Such a missionary congregation will have to include in its programme a continued renewal of its own life, proclamation, dialogue, service of the needy, projects to improve the relational life of the community, and action for social justice.[1]

No Christian congregation, however, is ever simply local. It is also a centre of world mission, part of that international, ecumenical network of communications which enlarge and enrich its own understanding of the fullness of the gospel. No longer is it the rare privilege of a few remote travellers to keep us in touch with the church on the other side of the world. Today God gives more and more of us the opportunity of meeting with people of other races, other cultures, other insights as they cross the world and come to live among us, opening up our local churches to wider horizons. There is good point in the story of the missionary's little girl who came home with her family from Hong Kong and going for the first time to a suburban English congregation said, 'But this isn't a proper church; there are no Chinese here!' We need the presence of more Chinese, West Indian, African, Asian Christians to turn us into 'proper' churches demonstrating visibly the universality of the gospel. Every Christian who comes to us from abroad as a new immigrant, a foreign student, a lay man or woman temporarily employed here, or a missionary sent from another church should be specially welcomed as a reminder and sign of our commitment to the worldwide, apostolic company of which each local congregation is a part. Each newcomer too should be seen as a potential agent of change bringing to us new insights and understanding.

This means that the sending and receiving of missionaries needs to become a much more international and mutual operation than it has been before. The initials ESP stand now not only for extra-sensory-perception, but for a development which could well extend the perceptive powers of Christians across the world – the ecumenical sharing of personnel. This would operate very much along the lines of 'mission control' at Houston in the sense that it would be a drawing together of teams of people on the basis of the varied skills and expertise they could bring to share together in one particular project. Thus, some new urban development in Birmingham might call for a team which had experience in urban mission in Tokyo and Detroit, in Kingston and in Calcutta, bringing together a multi-racial, international group putting their energies and experience at the disposal of a local project, acting as resource people serving the local leadership.

Such an enterprise is but one of the new patterns of mission which emerge as we take seriously the role of the church as an agency of salvation across the world today. The realities of the world we live in require of the church a flexibility in its methods of approach which will make great demands on its present highly-structured mission operations, often leading to sacrificial acts and daring risks both at home and overseas. To take seriously the mission of a local congregation may mean transferring a greater degree of sovereignty and more control over funds from central denominational boards to local churches. It may mean also releasing resources for groups of Christians who share a particular vision of their task and wish to experiment in new forms of witness without having to conform to the norms of the majority. It may mean cross-fertilizing from one continent to another the seeds of productive experiments.

The church as a national body needs to make its witness within the nation, speaking to the life of that nation as an integral part of its culture, free to respond to the movement of the Holy Spirit within that particular *milieu*. On some occasions this may for a time require the absence of foreigners and total independence from foreign support. In some areas local people may call for a moratorium on the sending of missionaries or money in order that the church in that area may find its own selfhood and develop its own mission. When that happens the churches which have traditional links with such an area must learn to accept with grace and in trust the request that they keep their distance and let the church be, so that it too may work out its own salvation.

In other situations there may be occasions when a foreign mission agency itself decides to withdraw from an area because it seems to be serving mainly the interests of an oppressive power. We have already seen how the White Fathers decided on such withdrawal from Mozambique (see above p. 76). Each situation is unique and requires careful assessment of whether withdrawing or remaining is likely to contribute most in the struggle for justice and in the work of salvation. Whenever possible, consultation must be taken between the mission agency and the oppressed people. In some repressive situations this is virtually impossible since people are not free to say what they really think, but it is possible to assess where the main strength of the mission agency's support lies – with the oppressed or with the oppressors. The major question is to ask how far the preaching of the gospel of salvation is validated by the way the mission agency is using its resources and its freedom of action within its own country in such a way as to undermine the oppression and foster liberation. No one coming from outside the situation can ever achieve a people's liberation for them, but they can at least get out of the way rather than delay the day of liberation by continuing to serve the interests of the oppressive powers.

It remains fundamentally true that no church is ever fully autonomous or independent. We all acknowledge our interdependence within the world Christian fellowship. What is needed is that the churches themselves shall be saved from perpetuating patterns of domination and dependence so that they can work out more mature relationships with one another. For so long now overseas missions have been seen primarily in terms of missions from the powerful and wealthy nations of the world and have therefore reflected the economic inequalities and the political patterns of the world they operate in. Yet the very concepts of power and wealth are alien to the true understanding of the gospel. Western churches need then to be saved from the power that can so easily corrupt and distort their mission and must learn to receive from those who once seemed powerless a deeper understanding of the meaning of the gospel. New ways of sharing power, of expressing genuine and reciprocal partnership, are being shown to us.

One model is the experiment made by the Paris Evangelical Missionary Society, which has dissolved itself in order that the Evangelical Community for Apostolic Action, a larger community representing churches in Africa, the Pacific, France, Italy and Switzerland, may take its place. Its purpose is to carry forward and transform the former work of the Paris Society and to pioneer new projects together. The Council, formed by the presidents of the participating churches, decides on the action to be undertaken and the use and deployment of funds and personnel placed at the disposal of the Community by the various churches. The

Council also engages in theological reflection which has resulted in directing questions to the churches of Europe regarding their own work and priorities.

What then is the relationship of missionary societies to the life of the churches in the world today? Perhaps the best answer is an analogy between the place of a missionary society within the life of its parent church and the place of the Division of World Mission and Evangelism within the life of the World Council of Churches. Just as it was the world missionary conference at Edinburgh in 1910 which woke up church leaders across the world to the need for them to stay together in the International Missionary Council, which was the beginning of the modern ecumenical movement, so a new missionary vision of the task of the church in our own land and throughout the world today would surely give us a new sense of urgency in our quest for unity. Just as the integration of that Missionary Council into the World Council of Churches has led to the recognition that the struggle against racism, the churches' participation in development, dialogue with people of other faiths, world mission and evangelism, are, equally with theological study and material relief, central to the obedient witness of Christians today, so in our own land a sustained sense of mission would compel us to realize that the planning going on in the town halls, the development of better community relations, the provision of adequate housing, the quality of entertainment offered by the mass media are all of paramount concern to Christians who want to witness to the reality of the gospel. It is as we are obedient to our Lord's command to take the gospel into all the world that we confront within that world the powers and principalities which are a denial of the gospel we proclaim.

Moreover, it is in mission that we discover most fully the scandal of our disunity which again is a denial of the reconciling power of the gospel. Many of the things that keep us Christians apart from one another are the same things that are tearing apart the life of the world. Questions of the true nature of authority, questions of the relative value of tradition and of present experience, questions of what are the essentials of a faith that can give meaning to life, above all a quest for a reconciliation which can enable us to accept the one who is different from us in such a way that that very difference can supply that which is lacking in our own understanding and experience, all these are issues that are relevant not only to schemes of church union but also to the search for salvation in the world today.

As Philip Potter, retiring as Director of the Commission on World Mission and Evangelism and taking up his post as General Secretary of the World Council of Churches, said in his report at Bangkok:

> But as we learned from the beginning of the ecumenical move-
> ment, the issues of unity and mission are inextricably bound
> together. More specifically the concern for church union and
> the emphasis on Joint Action for Mission are being tackled
> together. We have long spoken of the whole church with the
> whole gospel to the whole man in the whole world. The logic
> of this dictum, which was coined by such missionary statesmen
> as Hendrik Kraemer, demanded the effective integration of the
> ecumenical movement in its institutional form. It has certainly
> challenged the churches to rethink their missionary character
> and not leave missionary activity to para-ecclesiastical groups.
> It has also made more credible the understanding of mission as
> being on six continents and not just in one part of the world.
> Churches have been forced to find new and closer relations
> with missionary societies, as also with mission at home and
> abroad, to the neighbourhood and to the ends of the earth.[2]

The slogan of the Edinburgh Conference in 1910, led mainly by Westerners whose eyes were set on the ends of the earth, was 'the evangelization of the world in this generation'. Sixty years later in Bangkok, where the pace was set by those from the East and the South, whose eyes have shared the vision of a world redeemed by Christ, the slogan was echoed but restated in its contemporary expression – Salvation Today, through one mission together in a divided world.

What are the great divisions of our modern world? No longer are they to be thought of strictly in geographical or national terms, but rather in terms of economics, of politics and of faith. In every land today there are, as Disraeli said of

Victorian Britain, two nations, the nation of those who have and of those who have not. In every human institution there are to be found the powerful and the powerless. In every culture there are those who have found their way to faith and hope, and those who are lost in doubt and despair. In every generation there are the active and the apathetic. It is in the context of these different worlds that Christians are called together to witness to the offer of salvation.

Philip Potter's report at Bangkok on 'Christ's Mission and Ours in Today's World' pointed to the striking paradoxes of the world situation in which we all now live. We are aware as never before of living in one world, drawn together by speedy travel, rapid communication, universal commercialism. In Bangkok itself we felt this strongly. We saw all round us signs of what someone called the 'Coka-Colanization' of a city whose ancient temples are now hidden behind neon-lit advertisement hoardings. On the day of our arrival the Israeli Embassy of this Far-Eastern city was broken into by the Black September Movement of the Middle East confrontation. And through television our folks at home were seeing pictures of Bangkok as we arrived, long before our letters reached them. There has never been a more favourable time for getting a message out across the world. As Philip Potter put it:

> The fact of one world has held out great prospects for the world mission of the church. The eschatological words of Christ have become very vivid and urgent: 'This gospel of the Kingdom will be preached throughout the whole world (*oekumene*), as a testimony to the nations' (Matt. 24.14). This has created a lively debate in missionary circles as to whether the emphasis should be on proclaiming the gospel to the two billion or more who have never heard it in the lands which have lived for millenia by other faiths, or whether it should be preached literally to the whole world, including the so-called Christian lands of Europe, North America and Australasia. This debate is totally futile when we look closer at this one world in which we are living. Our one world is in reality a world which is profoundly divided politically, economically and racially.[3]

Straddling across the world like modern Colossi are the

giant powers of today in mortal conflict with one another, putting their big feet into the smaller but even more bloody conflicts of lesser powers. The fact that the one side wears the mask of atheistic communism and the other the mask of Christendom does nothing to commend either of their ideologies to those whom they trample underfoot.

These political divisions are inextricably related to economic realities. The giants hold in their hands vastly superior scientific and technological resources which have been constantly used to exploit even further the poverty of their victims. So despite massive efforts throughout the 1960s to redress the imbalance in the world by seeking to increase the economic development of poorer nations, despite all the emphasis placed by the United Nations and by other international bodies and notably by the churches on development and peace, the poor have become poorer and the rich become richer, until the whole concept of what is meant by development must be called in question. If development is based simply on what Philip Potter called 'the philosophy of aggressive individual and corporate egotism', then inevitably only the fittest can survive, and the poor go to the wall. A massive change of heart – a miraculous *metanoia* – is needed regarding what are the real values if there is to be any change of direction in the economic future of our world. It is in the realm of economics that many of the real questions arise as to how we can be saved. I remember a friend of mine who works in the Treasury going from a meeting of the Methodist Conference to a consultation of economists in Brussels and commenting afterwards, 'In the Conference we were discussing the structures of the church. At the consultation we were discussing the meaning and values of human life – what do we mean by "growth", by "standard of living", by development? As a Christian layman I have become more conscious of doing theology in my job than in my church life.' Economics has become a vital area for raising questions relating to mission today.

Another acid test of the reality of Christian claims is the reaction of Christians to the world-wide virus of racism. In the past, Western missionary enthusiasm has often been associated with a subtle sense of white superiority which has reinforced the latent racial prejudice in every human heart. From our earliest Sunday School days, many of us had impressed upon us so deeply the needs of 'poor black people' who needed our help that we accommodated ourselves easily to the concepts of white imperialism, which suggested that our land was a land of hope and glory for all peoples whom God had made mighty and would go on to make mightier yet. Only of recent years has the scandal of such heresy really been made plain to us, though from the earliest days of the ecumenical movement, our prophets have warned us of its dangers. Three years after the founding of the International Missionary Council. J. H. Oldham wrote his momentous book on *Christianity and the Race Problem*[4] in which he said:

> Christianity is not primarily a philosophy but a crusade. As Christ was sent by the Father, so he sends his disciples to set up in the world the Kingdom of God. His coming was a declaration of war – a war to the death against the powers of darkness. He was manifested to destroy the works of the devil. Hence when Christians find in the world a state of things that is not in accord with the truth which they have learned from Christ, their concern is not that it should be explained but that it should be ended. In that temper we must approach everything in the relations between races that cannot be reconciled with the Christian ideal.

So a programme to combat racism has become another vital area of Christian mission today, whether that racism is expressed in prejudiced inter-personal relations or enshrined in unjust political and economic systems. At Bangkok there was ample evidence that the help that the World Council of Churches has given in recent years to those organizations which are struggling for justice for oppressed peoples has restored for many Christians in Africa and Asia the whole credibility of the gospel. There has probably been no action that has spoken so eloquently of Christ's concern for the oppressed, of the relevance of Christian mission, of the universality of the gospel. And there has probably been no action that has so profoundly disturbed white Christians into a new look at the full meaning of their faith. A white Rhodesian once complained to me, 'The trouble with the churches is that they give the blacks big ideas.' Indeed they do – the biggest idea of all, the idea of the whole of humanity redeemed and liberated by Jesus Christ.

The second paradox to which Philip Potter pointed is that experienced between man's greatly increased power over creation through automation, the computer and the vast resources of science and technology and, at the same time, his increasing powerlessness to change effectively the structures of his society. Ten years ago we were learning to celebrate the idea of 'The Secular City' when theologians bade us rejoice in man come of age, entrusted with the power to develop a new environment for himself. We saw that secularization is not alien to the biblical emphasis on man's responsibility, but there are two other biblical insights we were in danger of ignoring:

> The first is that the whole point of the biblical revelation is that man should become responsible for himself and for his neighbour, and not place the blame on nature or on his heritage, or call on God in desperation to fill in the gaps or be a *deus ex machina*. The Bible is the story of the dialogue between God and man, and the purpose of God is to enable man to be responsible, to respond for himself and his neighbour before him. That is precisely what science and technology have made evident. And what has emerged is the true character of man as both wrapped up in himself individually and collectively, and incapable of changing himself and his creation to ends which are beyond his own selfish concerns. The other biblical insight is man's inveterate tendency to treat his own creations as transcendent, permanent realities, to make idols of them which he worships and invests with eternity. Whether we call this ideology or simply idolatry, we are dealing with the same reality.[5]

The reaction to this modern idolatry has been an intensified search for new gods, a new religiosity which has recently become a worldwide phenomenon. In Japan, alongside phenomenal growth in economics and technical power there has been a rapid growth of new religions. In Europe and North Africa there have mushroomed various forms of spirituality, from transcendental meditation to new forms of black magic. In Africa and Latin America there has been a resurgence of spiritism or of independent churches, some escaping from, some protesting against the inhuman system under which they live. Everywhere, people in their powerlessness seek a new power. It is in this situation that the power of the gospel, holding together as it does a concern for this world with a concern for ultimate and transcendent realities, comes with new force as a message of salvation.

The third paradox of which Philip Potter speaks is the paradox of the growth of counter-cultures. In some areas of the world the last decades have seen massive cultural revolutions, where determined attempts have been made to change radically the character of a whole people towards a renewed sense of communal responsibility. In other parts of the world there has been the development, particularly among young people, of a counter culture, calling in question all the values of the society in which they have grown up. Here is not a threat to evangelism, but a new thrust for it.

Carmencita Karagdag, a young Christian from the Philippines, sees this growth of a new counter-consciousness as a healthy sign, even though it is creating within the Christian church a growing division between those who see their role as supporting the *status quo* and those who in the old prophetic tradition have read the signs of the times and denounce oppression and exploitation. Speaking at the meeting of the World Council of Churches Central Committee in Utrecht in August 1972 she said:

If there is very little fellowship within the Christian world this is primarily because the world of humanity itself is profoundly divided. This division, this absence of fellowship, will last as long as we are as men, not necessarily as Christians, divided between oppressor and oppressed. Perhaps there is in this growing polarization the very action of God in trying to break the bondage of his people. Perhaps Christians can start moving along the road to genuine reconciliation and fellowship, not by hastily patching up gaping wounds by the uneasy peace of compromise, not by glossing over the contradictions between the developed and underdeveloped countries by any false arguments of peace and universality, but by seriously taking their whole situation to the cross through a confession of participation in injustice. Through repentance and shame; through suffering with Christ; more concretely perhaps by rejecting the conservative ideologies to which we are presently wed and which prevent us from truly feeling with those who suffer, and by adopting a new religious counter-consciousness that is truly for and of the people, that really serves the interest of those with whom Christ suffered. Short of this I fear that Christianity will remain an obstacle to genuine liberation, a force of reaction that cannot but be swept away by the forces of history.[6]

So in this one world, in all six continents, we perceive the many divided worlds of politics and economics, of nation and race, of secular achievement and religious awareness, of cultural revolution and counter-cultural protest. It is in these divided worlds that we hear with new emphasis our Lord's command – 'Go into *all* the world and preach the gospel' – and in obedience to that command we are bound to be all together now.

9

On the Receiving End

Salvation in Britain Today

Is there any gospel for the rich? We have seen clearly how the gospel is understood literally as good news for the poor, and how in the poorer nations of the world people see the salvation offered in Christ in specific terms of their own situation. The fruits of salvation would be liberation in South Africa, or independence in Angola, or healing in India, or peace in Vietnam. But what would salvation mean in the affluent, Western world? Is there good news for the rich?

One stark answer stands out on the pages of the New Testament. To the rich young ruler the call of Jesus was uncompromising. 'Go and sell what you have and give to the poor and come and follow me' (Luke 18.18–30). From Zacchaeus, the tax collector, the response was equally practical. 'The half of my goods I give to the poor and if I have robbed any man I restore to him fourfold', a response which was met with the declaration, 'Today is salvation come to this house' (Luke 19.2–10). Is it all as simple as that? Get rid of your riches, make reparation for your wrongs and you will find salvation? The irony is that even when we do attempt ever so slightly to obey such simple commandments, we tend to think in terms not of our salvation but of the salvation of others. We give reasonably generously to Christian Aid in the hope thereby of enriching the poor; we send money to a fund to combat racism in an attempt to liberate the oppressed, and still fail to see that it is we who are most enriched by such giving and we who most need liberation. If the rich young ruler had had the courage to obey Jesus, even all his riches would have made precious little difference to the poor but the loss of them would have made a world of difference to him, for then he would have found the treasure in heaven.

If all this seems too simple in the complex economics of our modern world, perhaps one thing to which the gospel is recalling Western Christians is a new simplicity of life. The growing contrast between rich and poor is critical not only because of the deprivation suffered by those who are poor but also because of the degradation which is fast distorting any sense of value in affluent societies. The pollutions, both material and moral, caused by wealth are now as grave a danger to the future of mankind as the sicknesses of poverty. To refuse to mount any higher up the spiral of rising expectations might be one very simple way in which Christians in the Western world could demonstrate that in their life-style it is Jesus who sets the pace rather than the Joneses. One of the most effective statements to come out of the British Church Leaders' Conference held in September 1972 was also the simplest. It called British Christians to a new simplicity of living and did so in a series of straightforward but searching questions which we ought to ask ourselves as world citizens today:

- How can we measure our real needs – by the standards of our neighbours or by the needs of the poor?
- How can we be joyful without being greedy or flamboyant, for example, in hospitality?
- How far does our personal way of life depend on society's wealth? Can our society's way of life be simpler? Is there any one such change we ourselves can work for?
- How can we be good stewards without being over-scrupulous? What decisions about personal life are the decisive ones to make – for example, budgeting, family size, etc.?

– How can others benefit from what we have, our house,
    our car and our possessions?
To these questions were added points to ponder:
  – Happiness is knowing what I can do without.
  – My greed is another's need.
  – Am I detached from worldly goods if I keep what I have
    and want to add to them?[1]

Another saving grace in Western society today would be
the recovery of spirituality. I use that word not primarily in
terms of devotional exercise or mystical experience, but
rather in the sense in which M. M. Thomas used it in his
definition of spirituality as that which distinguishes human
beings from animals, giving them power to make choices, to
transcend their immediate needs and to find ultimate meaning and sacredness in all their striving. The recovery of a
true spirituality would release us from the current unnatural
obsessions of Western society with two natural processes, sex
and death. Pornography is obscene, not because it portrays
a physical function, but because it robs that function of any
meaning, separating it from the sacredness of relationship.
The concentration on violence is degrading not simply because it encourages aggression but because it cheapens life
and robs death of any kind of dignity or reverence. Two of
the lessons we most need to learn in the West today are how
to love wisely and how to die well. The facts of life and the
facts of death are both too often presented in such dehuman-
ized terms that they are robbed of their deepest spiritual
values and thereby prevented from being themselves ways to
salvation.
    Even in a growing concern for man's physical environ-
ment, there is often an alarming lack of awareness of people's
need to participate in shaping their own destiny. Not far
from where I live in London is an area whose very heart is
being torn out to make way for what is termed 'urban
renewal'. A largely residential area in a long-standing community of tall gracious houses and compact streets has been
bulldozed to make way for wider roads and high-rise tene-
ment blocks. The community has been utterly disrupted,

bed-sitters and overnight lodging places have totally disappeared, the whole character of the neighbourhood changed in a way which none of the local residents either desired or designed. No doubt the planners had good intentions, but what seems so deplorable is the lack of any real consultation with those whose whole life-style will have to change and who are made to feel that they are entirely the victims of processes against which they are helpless, and therefore have lost their humanity.

Similarly, even the services offered by the welfare state seem often singularly lacking in any real respect for human capacities. In a report describing the Peter Bedford Project, which has pioneered recently in ways of enabling homeless and rootless people to form communities of their own and support themselves by their own efforts, Michael Sorensen writes:

> There are now probably ten times as many officials concerned in rehabilitating offenders as there were ten years ago, and ten times as much money is being spent by them. But the rate of recidivism has increased and so, we are told, has the number of homeless men. As in housing, the gathering of increasing skills and equipment and other resources has not solved a problem and is possibly even creating new problems of its own. And in both cases this is not through any lack of good intention.
>
> The lack in both cases is rather of respect for real human needs and capacities. So far as prisons are concerned, and prison aftercare, the object of the effort is treated, and publicly described, as a poor wretched fellow who is in need of pity and support and cash. He may well be in some need of these, and yet it is death to think so or to let him think so, for what he needs more than anything is to believe that he is not. When he has started to walk, support and backing can well fall into place behind him, as they must; but if they are brought into play too soon, or on the wrong terms, they can well stop him from ever learning to walk at all.[2]

'In the name of Jesus Christ, get up and walk', said Peter and John in one of the first great acts of salvation recorded in the Book of Acts (Acts 3.1–10). One of the great debates in Britain today is what we do with the 'lame ducks' of our society. One expression of salvation would be to give them back through the right kind of compassion and of concentrated energy the power to get up on their feet again.

This would mean Christians becoming much more active in the struggle for social justice in this land and throughout the world than they have been recently. We point with pride in our history to the witness of the Tolpuddle Martyrs and the origins of the Trade Union Movements, to the Clapham Sect and the Abolition of Slavery campaign, to the Nonconformist Conscience and the Education Acts of this century, but where does the church display the same kind of energy in relation to the parallel movements today? What priority do Trade Union meetings have for Christians in industry? How many churches actively support Anti-Apartheid? To what extent have Christians pioneered a concern for the growing numbers of homeless people in this decade? What is the real understanding of Christian vocation with regard to the teaching profession? The world of industry, of race relations, of housing, of education all need to be seen by Christians as arenas of salvation.

Perhaps the nearest we have come to mobilizing Christian forces in any social action in recent times was the Sign-In held by Christian Aid at Christmas 1969, when over a million signatures were collected for a petition to the Government to increase the official aid given from this country to the promised 1% of the Gross National Product. Such activity, backed as it was by a programme of education and concern, ought to be the norm of our church life rather than an extraordinary event.

All this would depend on the recovery by the churches in the West of a true sense of mission in their own lands. It was notable that at Bangkok the representatives from most Asian and African countries were concerned with mission within their own nations, while most of those who came from the West, especially from Britain and the USA, were mainly from bodies concerned with mission overseas. Western nations were still seen as the bases for sending mission rather than the field for mission operations in themselves. True, there were reports of special mission campaigns – Call to the North, Action North West, Key 73 and so on, but there seemed little evidence of churches being totally mobilized for mission as their normal on-going programme of activity. People from the West expressed little expectation of church growth, either in terms of numerical membership or of spiritual strength. The prevailing mood was one of decline and even despair, so that one began to feel that the unexpected reticence of Western delegates at the Conference was not so much due to a new-found humility on the part of Western Christians, which some offered as an explanation, but even to a feeling of spiritual bankruptcy. When it came to questions about how far the gospel was being effectively proclaimed in our own lands today we were unusually silent because we had nothing to say.

This is where it became apparent that the gospel is indeed not only good news for the poor, but good news from the poor too. The messengers of faith, of hope and of love in today's world are to be found not so much in places of long Christian tradition and of present secular affluence as among those for whom the gospel is still news, for whom future hope transcends present reality, for whom love transforms oppressive suffering. D. T. Niles used to say that every Christian, in order that his faith be rekindled, ought to have at least one friend who is a first-generation believer. A parallel to that would be to plead that every Western church, in order to revitalize the true heart of its mission, ought to have a blood transfusion from the life of the younger churches.

Such a life-saving transfusion could mean a transformation of the churches in the West. For one thing, it would quicken the impulse towards church unity. There was a time when we in Britain used to imagine that churches throughout the rest of the world were waiting anxiously for the outcome of union negotiations here in order to determine their own ecumenical future. Regarding ourselves as the mother churches of great world communions, and moreover the originators of many of the quarrels that have divided Christendom, we attached universal significance to our local schemes of union between, for instance, the Church of England and the Methodist Church of Great Britain. Perhaps we needed the lesson of humility when the failure of that scheme was followed by news of the successful consummation of unions in Sri-Lanka, in North India and in many other parts of the world, where the urgency of mission had given the younger churches an impetus to unity which leaves mother far behind, still fussing about her household affairs. From that lesson let us hope that we have now learned to include within any discussions of future ecumenical relations in Britain consultation with representatives of those churches which are already enjoying the fruits of union.

Another life-saving gift which would come to us as we became more ready to receive from other parts of the world would be both a rediscovery of our own cultural heritage and the enrichment of the diversity of other cultures. Enoch Powell once gave a strong warning to Britain that the presence of many immigrants of other races within this nation would profoundly disturb our traditional cultural patterns. That is something that Christians see as a promise rather than a threat. Here is the promise of a new vitality, a rich variety that could transform a tired society. One sees evidence of it everywhere today. Walk down any London street and see the exciting variety of fashion – caftans and dashikis, trousers and saris, African cloths and Indian silks, American denims and Paris couture. Look at the restaurants and see the exotic choice of menus – curry and rice, bean shoots and noodles or fish and chips according to taste! Who would want to return to the uniformity and monotony of pre-war Britain?

Yet it has to be admitted that for many people in this country, the proximity of so many new neighbours has brought the same kind of cultural shock as initially overcomes most travellers to a new continent. Beyond that shock lies all the thrill of new discovery. Once people can learn to accept the new, the different, the other not as a threat but as an enrichment, a whole new world opens up for them. In that sense, what we need most in this island community of ours is release from our fears of all that comes from beyond our borders and a new readiness to recognize that we who have for so long and with such confidence exported our styles, our values, our systems to the rest of the world now have much to gain by being on the receiving end. Here is an offer of liberation, the chance to let go of the awesome and arrogant British sense of responsibility for all the rest of the world. Now we have instead the opportunity to participate in the beginning of a new cultural as well as a new political history for the whole of mankind, in which we can learn what it really means to belong not to an empire, but to the family of man.

I can speak of that enrichment from my own personal experience of relationships shared across racial and cultural barriers. It is a West Indian working woman who has taught me most about the meaning of family responsibility; it is an African friend who has led me to a greater appreciation of the power of prayer; it is Indian neighbours who have shown me the graciousness of generous hospitality. And with all these gifts, each has given, albeit unconsciously, a greater gift still – the gift of acceptance which can forgive the sins I inherit from my white race and offers instead the privilege of reconciling friendship.

If this can happen in personal relationships, how much richer such an interchange would be between churches. There are so many ways in which Christians bringing insights from overseas could clarify things for us here. They would help us to distinguish more clearly the difference between what belongs to our culture as Britishers and what is essential to our commitment as Christians. They would help us to reassess the priorities of our church's life, to discover what it really does mean to be a church in mission. They would help us to think and act ecumenically in the fullest meaning of that word. I have often noticed that in this country when we say 'we must act ecumenically' we usually mean 'at the pace of the other churches in this land', whereas the word ought to mean in fellowship with the whole church across the world, in a shared concern for the whole inhabited earth. And when we try to hear ourselves through the ears of our African brethren or to see ourselves through the eyes of Asian Christians, we begin to develop a new sensitivity and to see a new viewpoint.

Best of all, the transformation that would come with the

transfusion of new spirituality from overseas would express itself in new ways of worshipping. One thing Westerners need to learn from the East and the South is the way to celebrate life. Whether it be a birth or a funeral, a wedding or a parting, life and love are to be affirmed and celebrated. I have been to many a West Indian party in London which has mingled prayer and dancing, religious hymns and reggae music with such spontaneous joy that I have felt renewed by both. Indeed I have found that the only people who do not enjoy West Indian parties are those who have never been to them! Yet we have to learn together ways of bringing that same spontaneous joy into our more formal services of worship, some of which have been in the past under our influence quite as lifeless among predominantly West Indian congregations as they are among our own. But today the spirit seems to be pouring out his new gifts upon us all. We are discovering together the joys of worship, as he takes the richness of our shared traditions and brings out things new and old from such a treasure store.

It was like that not so long ago at a never-to-be-forgotten service in St Martin-in-the-Fields. The occasion was a requiem for Martin Luther King. The choirmaster and organizer was the renowned West Indian musician, Ian Hall. The choir were London University students. The first half included the solemn classical music of Fauré's Requiem, the second half began with an African solo funeral dance; it ended with the whole congregation, African and Asian, West Indian and British dancing together in the aisles of that city church to the words of William Blake, affirming gladly 'Everything that lives is holy'.

That recovery of wholeness, that recall to a true spirituality, that rediscovery of one another – all this is offered to us as we learn to receive more readily and more humbly those who have so much to give us from other parts of the world. We who are so rich in things and so poor in spirit, we too need the gospel. And as we receive it from fellow Christians all over the world we shall find restored to us too the joy of our salvation.

10

What a Hope!

Salvation and the Future

There can be no end to a book on salvation. Salvation lies beyond the end. Everything that has been said so far in this book has been anticipatory. The rediscovery of personal identity, the affirmation of cultural heritage, the struggle for social justice, the renewal of churches for mission, all these are but ways in which the church is called to live in and for a future salvation which lies beyond each person's death and beyond the consummation of all our human history. No human life is complete this side of the grave. No human system can claim to offer the ultimate salvation of man. Only the transcendent realities of eternity can transform the present realities of the here and now, as men and women who have seen a vision of the salvation that belongs to God become the inspired agents of that salvation in their local situation and in their own day.

So we come back to where we began. Salvation is ultimately about the reality of God, and the victory that is his beyond all that would seem to deny his power and destroy his purpose. The first Christians lived face to face with death but their faith in the salvation that lay beyond their final death enabled them to die daily to their immediate sufferings and to live in the power of resurrection life. For many of us today, the refusal to look death in the face robs us of the reality of that resurrection experience. Death relativizes life. Tidying up the affairs of a person who had died puts new perspective on all that person lived for. What will be saved out of it all? The money – of no value to him now. The property – standing empty. The clothes – to be cast away. But the faith and the hope and the love by which he lived – these surely are vindicated, these are of eternal value, these are saved as his life reaches its ultimate meaning beyond the grave, in the salvation that belongs to our God.

What we believe to be true of an individual we believe to be true also for the whole universe. The threats of destruction of much of our world's fabric are no doubt as inevitable as the threat of death itself, but the faith and the hope and the love that are let loose in the world today are the heralds of that total, cosmic salvation which will restore creation and redeem mankind. To preach salvation today then, means to hold fast that faith, to live by that hope, to enact that love in joyful affirmation, celebrating here and now the gift of God which is eternal life in Jesus Christ. This was the theme of an affirmation written by one of the groups at Bangkok. With their words, followed by the prayers and praises that came out of the Conference,[1] let this book end and the readers' response begin.

Affirmation on Salvation Today

With gratitude and joy we affirm again
our confidence in the sufficiency of our crucified and risen Lord.
We know him as the one who is, and who was, and who is to come,
the sovereign Lord of all.

To the individual he comes with power
to liberate him from every evil and sin,
from every power in heaven and earth,
and from every threat of life or death.

To the world he comes as the Lord of the universe,
with deep compassion for the poor and the hungry,

to liberate the powerless and the oppressed.
To the powerful and the oppressors he comes
in judgment and mercy.

We see God at work today
both within the church and beyond the church
towards the achievement of his purpose
that justice might shine on every nation.

He calls his church to be part of his saving activity
both in calling men to decisive personal response to his
Lordship,
and in unequivocal commitment to the movements and
works
by which all men may know justice
and have opportunity to be fully human.

In joyous trust in Christ's power and victory
we can live with freedom and hope
whatever the present may be.

The Lord is at hand.

Celebrating Salvation

Prayers and Meditations from the Bangkok Conference

An Affirmation of Faith

We came from almost too many situations,
with the usual prejudice, our own ideas, our exaggerated
hopes,
many of us tired of conferences, all of us full of our own
preoccupations.

Then we shared our biographical materials, struggling to
express our thoughts, groping for words that might
communicate,
hurting each other by hasty reactions, being hurt when not
heard,
showing some of the frustrations we have in our work back
home,
sharing our fear for the future of the world, our feeble faith.

And in that process we were met by God himself,
who revealed himself in his Word, which we studied,
in our friends around the table who questioned us,
who gave us new insights, comforted us, accepted our
limitations.

Not more than a glimpse of God we saw,
a smile of his grace,
a gentle gesture of judgment.

And so we repented, because we saw that God is so much
greater than we.
We experienced the meek force of God's invitation to
continuous conversion:
and we accepted to be sent back whence we came,
a little better motivated, a little wiser, a little sadder,
a little closer to him.

A Prayer of Praise

We praise you, God our Father, for the wild riches of your
creation
for the uniqueness of each person,
for the creativity, sustaining and renewing our
cultures,
for your faithfulness towards your people.

We praise you, Jesus our Lord, for your constant meddling
in our affairs,
for your identification with the poor,
for your sacrifice for all men on the cross,
for revealing the true man to all people.

We praise you, God the Spirit, for your inspiration of life,
for your translation of the anguish of creation,
for your insistence to draw us always to Christ,
for the infusion of unrest among man,
for your patient preparation of the fulfilment of
history.

We praise you, blessed Trinity, for not doing to us
according to our sins,
for continuing your love to all that lives,
for continuing your disturbing call to repentance,
for continuing life on earth. Amen.

A Prayer of Intercession

For people caught in exploration,
neglected by systems, raped by ideologies,
caught between machines, shrivelled up by loneliness,
hardened by their convictions, deaf for surprises,
blind for suffering, crippled by unfreedom,
we pray: Out of the depths we cry unto thee, O Lord!
For Christ's church on earth,
confused about its message, uncertain about its role,
divided in many days, polarised between different
                                        understandings,
unimaginative in its proclamation, undisciplined in its
                                        fellowship,
we pray: Out of the depths we cry unto thee, O Lord!
For ourselves in this conference,
overwhelmed by our impressions, torn apart by prejudice,
often in doubt, plagued by frustrations,
struggling for honesty, for understanding of each other,
crying for love, searching for justice,
we pray: Out of the depths we cry unto thee, O Lord!

Some Meditations

Lord, show us deeply how important it is to be useless.
Lord, teach us the silence of humility
        the silence of wisdom
        the silence of love
        the silence that speaks without words
        the silence of faith.
Lord, teach us to silence our own hearts and minds
        that we may listen to the movement of the Holy Spirit
        within us and sense the depths which are God.

Who am I?
        I am the people I met
        I am the books I studied
        I am the joy I experienced
        I am the suffering I see
        I am the longing for something better to come soon.

What am I to do?
  I try to identify
  I try to be critical
  I try to bring about some change
  I try to love
  I try to learn from Jesus how to live.
I am glad he came.

A Litany

God of Moses, saved in the river;
God of Israel, freed from Egypt, freed from the desert;
God of the slain Lamb, powerless Lion of Judah;
God of Brazil, of the millions exploited by the black magic
                                        of growth;
God of Mexico, of the ambivalence of the revolution;
God of New York, of disappointment and of new life;
God of the theologians, deceived by the wind of
                                        doctrine;
God of the bureaucrats, nervously searching for new
                                        programmes;
God of Africa, of a growing church in a land of
                                        exploitation;
God of the religious people, caught in the projection of
                                        their own mind;
God of the conservatives, of the burning desire to save
                                        souls;

God of the liberals, dreaming of reform;
God of the radicals, dreaming of revolution;
God of the artists, creativity of man;
God of the technocrats, enslaved to the power they hold;
God of the exploiters, love of power;
God of the Christians, between faith and unfaith;
God of those who have never heard of Jesus Christ;
God of those who have heard of Christ but only see his
                                        people;

God of us – God of all men,
    surprise us anew with your faithfulness, save us today!

A Litany of Praise and Prayer

O God,
You have called us out of death, we praise you!
    Send us back with the bread of life, we pray you!
You have turned us around, we praise you!
    Keep us faithful, we pray you!
You have begun a good work, we praise you!
    Complete your salvation in us, we pray you!
You have made us a chosen people, we praise you!
    Make us one with all people, we pray you!
You have taught us your law, we praise you!
    Change us by the Spirit's Power, we pray you!
You have sent your Son in one place and time, we praise
        you!
    Be present in every time and place, we pray you!
Your Kingdom has come in His salvation, we praise you!
    Let it come always among us, we pray you! Amen.

Notes

IRM – International Review of Mission
Many of the poems and articles quoted are collected together in
the anthology *Salvation Today and Contemporary Experience*, an issue
of *Risk* (Vol. 9, No. 3) published by the World Council of Churches
in preparation for the Conference.

Chapter 1
1. Used by permisson of the author. Translation by the World
Council of Churches.
2. From *Kurukshetram*. Used by permission of the author.
3. M. M. Thomas, 'Salvation and Humanization', *IRM*, January
1971, p. 34.
4. Fourth Assembly of the World Council of Churches, 1968, *The
Uppsala Report*, WCC 1968, p. 27.

Chapter 2
1. Marguerite Yourcenar, *L'Oeuvre au Noir*, Editions Alphée,
Monaco: English text under the title *Opus Nigrum*, translated
from the French by Grace Frick in collaboration with the author,
to be publised shortly by Weidenfeld & Nicolson.
2. A-M. Aagaard, 'No One Needs Saving From Love', Cyclostyled Paper, WCC 1973, pp. 1, 3f.
3. Julian of Norwich, *Revelations of Divine Love*, ch. 86; Penguin
ed., tr. Cliton Wolters.
4. From a song by Sydney Carter, 'Friday Morning', in *In the Present
Tense*, Galliard Ltd 1969. © Galliard Ltd 1969. Reprinted by
permission.

Chapter 3
1. Benjamin Uffenheimer, in 'Biblical Essays on Salvation', Cyclostyled Paper, WCC 1972, p. 4.

2. Samuel Amirtham, in 'Biblical Essays on Salvation', p. 8.
3. Ibid., p. 14.

Chapter 4

1. Philip Potter, 'Sermon at Geneva Cathedral', Central Committee Paper, WCC 1973.
2. Kenneth Grayston, in 'Biblical Essays on Salvation', p. 25.
3. Ibid., p. 30.
4. Ibid., pp. 36ff.

Chapter 5

1. 'Reflections on the Conference', Cyclostyled Paper Ed Doc. No. 44, WCC 1973, p. 4.
2. Ibid., p. 5.
3. Emilio Castro, 'Bangkok, the New Opportunity', *IRM*, April 1973, p. 136.
4. Rubem A. Alves, 'Mission in an Apocalyptic Era', Cyclostyled Paper, WCC 1973, pp. 2, 4f, 7f.
5. M. M. Thomas, 'The Meaning of Salvation Today – A Personal Statement', *IRM*, April 1973, pp. 164f.

Chapter 6

1. Tony Parker, *People of the Streets*, Jonathan Cape 1968.
2. From a song by Sydney Carter, 'The Mask I Wore', in *In the Present Tense*, Galliard Ltd 1969. © Galliard Ltd 1969. Reprinted by permission.
3. N. V. Tilak, tr. Nicol Macnicol, *The Methodist Hymn Book*, No. 159, The Methodist Publishing House, 1933.
4. Bangkok Conference Section I, 'Culture and Identity', *IRM*, April 1973, p. 188.
5. Gabriel Setiloane, 'I am an African', Pro Veritate Ltd, Transvaal, SA.
6. 'Culture and Identity', *IRM*, April 1973, pp. 185, 186.
7. Stanley Samartha, 'Dialogue as a Continuing Christian Concern', *The Ecumenical Review*, April 1971, pp. 138f., reprinted in *Living Faiths and the Ecumenical Movement*, ed. S. J. Samartha, WCC 1971, pp. 153–4.
8. Roger Garaudy, *L'homme de Nazareth*. From a review article, reproduced by permission of the author. English translation by the World Council of Churches.
9. 'Report of Section I, Bangkok Conference', Cyclostyled Paper, WCC 1973.

Chapter 7

1. Bangkok Conference Section II, 'Salvation and Social Justice', *IRM*, April 1973, p. 199.
2. Ibid., p. 204.
3. The American Task Force, 'The Relation of Mission Boards to the Angolan People', *IRM*, April 1973, p. 202.
4. Harold Good and Meiriad Corrigan, 'Action Report on Northern Ireland submitted to the Bangkok Conference', January 1973.
5. 'Statement on Salvation and Indo-China', WCC January 1973.

Chapter 8

1. Bangkok Conference Section III, 'Churches Renewed in Mission', *IRM*, April 1973, p. 217.
2. Philip Potter, 'Christ's Mission and Ours in Today's World', *IRM*, April 1973, p. 153.
3. Ibid., p. 145.
4. SCM Press 1924.
5. Philip Potter, art. cit., p. 150.
6. Carmencita Karagdag, 'Is Fellowship Possible?', *Ecumenical Review*, October 1972, p. 465.

Chapter 9

1. See David L. Edwards, *The British Churches Turn to the Future*, SCM Press 1973, p. 73.
2. Richard Grover and Michael Sorenson, *The Peter Bedford Project in 1972*, John Bellers Ltd 1973, p. 10.

Chapter 10

1. For more prayers and meditation from the Bangkok Conference see *IRM*, April 1973, pp. 194-7.